Mich...

The Spanish economy

New Studies in Economic and Social History

Edited for the Economic History Society by
Michael Sanderson
University of East Anglia, Norwich

This series, specially commissioned by the Economic History Society, provides a guide to the current interpretations of the key themes of economic and social history in which advances have recently been made or in which there has been significant debate.

In recent times economic and social history has been one of the most flourishing areas of historical study. This has mirrored the increasing relevance of the economic and social sciences both in a student's choice of career and in forming a society at large more aware of the importance of these issues in their everyday lives. Moreover specialist interests in business, agricultural and welfare history, for example, have themselves burgeoned and there has been an increased interest in the economic development of the wider world. Stimulating as these scholarly developments have been for the specialist, the rapid advance of the subject and the quantity of new publications make it difficult for the reader to gain an overview of particular topics, let alone the whole field.

New Studies in Economic and Social History is intended for students and their teachers. It is designed to introduce them to fresh topics and to enable them to keep abreast of recent writing and debates. All the books in the series are written by a recognised authority in the subject, and the arguments and issues are set out in a critical but unpartisan fashion. The aim of the series is to survey the current state of scholarship, rather than to provide a set of prepackaged conclusions.

The series has been edited since its inception in 1968 by Professors M. W. Flinn, T. C. Smout and L. A. Clarkson, and is currently edited by Dr Michael Sanderson. From 1968 it was published by Macmillan as *Studies in Economic History,* and after 1974 as *Studies in Economic and Social History.* From 1995 *New Studies in Economic and Social History* is being published on behalf of the Economic History Society by Cambridge University Press. This new series includes some of the titles previously published by Macmillan as well as new titles, and reflects the ongoing development throughout the world of this rich seam of history.

For a full list of titles in print, please see the end of the book.

The Spanish economy

From the Civil War to the European Community

Prepared for the Economic History Society by

Joseph Harrison
University of Manchester

CAMBRIDGE
UNIVERSITY PRESS

Published by the Press Syndicate of the University of Cambridge
The Pitt Building, Trumpington Street, Cambridge CB2 1RP
40 West 20th Street, New York, NY 10011-4211, USA
10 Stamford Road, Oakleigh, Melbourne 3166, Australia

The Economic History Society 1993
The Spanish Economy was first published by The Macmillan Press Limited
1993
First Cambridge University Press edition 1995

Printed in Great Britain at the University Press, Cambridge

A catalogue record for this book is available from the British Library

Library of Congress cataloguing in publication data

Harrison, Joseph, 1944–
The Spanish economy: from the Civil War to the European Community /
prepared for the Economic History Society by Joseph Harrison.
    p.   cm. – (New studies in economic and social history)
Includes bibliographical references and index.
ISBN 0 521 55281 8 (hc). – ISBN 0 521 55772 0 (pb)
1. Spain – Economic conditions – 20th century.
I. Economic History Society.
II. Title.   III. Series.
HC385.H335   1995   330.946'08–dc20   95–18079   CIP

ISBN 0 521 55281 8 hardback
ISBN 0 521 55772 0 paperback

CE

For Mary

Contents

List of tables	*page*	viii
Acknowledgements		ix
Map of Spain		x
1 Backwardness and progress, 1900–36		1
2 An outline of economic development since the Civil War		7
3 Demographic developments		20
4 Agriculture		26
5 Industry		33
6 Energy		42
7 The service sector		49
8 Foreign trade		53
9 The financial system		60
Concluding remarks		67
Bibliography		69
Index		76

Tables

1 Marriages, births and deaths, 1900–86
  (per thousand inhabitants)   22
2 The mechanisation of farms according to size
  of holdings, 1962–82   30

Acknowledgements

In my wanderings across the Iberian peninsula over the years, I have built up an enormous debt of gratitude to many Spanish scholars who took time to offer me intellectual sustenance. Above all, as far as this work is concerned, I wish to thank Carlos Barciela, Francisco Comín, José Luis Garcia Delgado, Manuel-Jesús González, Pablo Martín Aceña, Jordi Nadal, Jordi Palafox, Leandro Prados, Pedro Tedde, Ignasi Terradas and Gabriel Tortella. Once again, I gratefully acknowledge the marvellous hospitality provided me by the incomparable Casa de Velázquez in Madrid and its general secretary, Jean-Gérard Gorges. The British Academy and the Nuffield Foundation awarded me generous grants to carry out research in Barcelona and Madrid. Among the librarians who set me on the right tracks are those of the Biblioteca de Catalunya, Foment del Treball Nacional, Bank of Spain, Biblioteca Nacional and the Casa de Velázquez. In this country, Alan Milward and Paul Preston have always been an inspiration to me in my researches. Last but not least, Mary Harrison typed up the manuscript with patience, charm and good humour and saved me from many an error. Those which remain are entirely of my own making.

Map of Spain

1

Backwardness and progress, 1900–36

In July 1936, elements of Spain's armed forces, garrisoned in Morocco and parts of the Iberian peninsula staged a *coup d'état* against the democratically-elected government of the Second Republic. Not for the first time in modern Spanish history, the nation was plunged into a bloody civil war which divided its peoples, resulted in huge losses of human life and brought about the physical destruction of homes, factories and economic infrastructure. After almost three years of bitter conflict, the insurgents led by General Francisco Franco, who were backed by Hitler's Germany and Mussolini's Italy, emerged triumphant.

Within Spain, Franco's New Order enjoyed practically unanimous support from the military, landowners, big business, the banks and the Church. Urged on by the triumphalist rhetoric of the *Movimiento*, the single party of the one-party state, the new regime set about eliminating all opposition, whether it came from liberals, Marxists, anarchists, intellectuals, home rulers or any other source. Hard-won achievements such as parliamentary democracy, free trade unions, freedom of the press, agrarian reforms or the devolution of power to Catalonia and the Basque Country, were savagely repressed by the Francoist authorities. Put bluntly, post-civil war Spain comprised two groups: the victors and the vanquished. Motivated by a fierce desire for vengeance, the Franco dictatorship continued to execute its former opponents long after the ceasefire of April 1939. At the same time, to escape incarceration or the firing squad, tens of thousands of defeated Republicans and their families fled the country. Most of Spain's exiles were young and active. A country ready to embark on the process of reconstruction could ill afford to dispense with their skills.

For those who stayed behind, the spoils of war were not to be enjoyed by everyone. For the vast majority of peasants, rural labourers and factory workers, the 1940s was a decade of harvest failure, short-time work, water shortages, power cuts, hunger and rationing. Whatever meagre economic advance the governments of the Restoration Monarchy (1874–1931) and the Second Republic (1931–9) had presided over, in the fields and workshops of Franco's Spain, the dictatorship became a by-word for misery, retardation and abject failure in just about every facet of economic life, apart from a thriving black market. Thanks largely to its mismanagement of economic affairs, little improvement took place before the appearance of faltering growth in the 1950s.

An agrarian society

Early twentieth century Spain was an overwhelmingly agricultural society. At the turn of the century, two out of every three Spaniards worked on the land, a proportion which had varied little since the beginning of the previous century. By comparison, the level of urbanisation south of the Pyrenees was remarkably low. In 1900, only nine per cent of the population lived in cities with over one hundred thousand inhabitants.

The traditional view of the Spanish countryside in the period 1900–36 is one of stagnation and routine. After a widespread agricultural crisis which hit the basic staples of Mediterranean agriculture (wheat, the vine, olives) in the late nineteenth century, large numbers quit the soil. Hundreds of thousands emigrated, mainly to Latin America. After 1887, successive governments reacted to the threat to the livelihoods of the nation's farmers by awarding the most powerful lobbies, not least the cereal growers of Old Castile, hefty doses of tariff protection against cheap imports – the main cause of the crisis. Meanwhile, little was attempted to stimulate the cultivation of other crops in which Spain possessed a comparative advantage in world markets.

Recent research, however, rejects the previously held viewpoint of agrarian immobilism. Despite the absence of a fully-fledged policy for agriculture, the first third of the present century is stated to have witnessed hitherto unacknowledged progress in the

Spanish countryside. The Grupo de Estudios de Historia Rural contend that between 1900 and 1931 agricultural production expanded by 55 per cent, an average of 1.4 per cent per annum, more than twice that of neighbouring France though starting from a lower base. From 1910 to 1922, according to the group's calculations, it grew by a yearly rate of 2.13 per cent. Within the agricultural sector, livestock farming grew by 123 per cent in the first three decades of the century, a clear reflection of improved living standards. The same period was also characterised by the spread of a number of new products, including oranges, almonds, potatoes, sugar beet and horticultural products. Certain of these crops, like citrus fruit, responded to an increase in foreign demand. Exports of oranges, most notably from the *País Valenciano*, constituted one of the principal sources of income for the Spanish economy in the 1920s. In contrast, the expansion of sugar beet cultivation, centred on Aragon and Andalusia, was largely due to burgeoning internal demand following the loss of Cuba, with its influential sugar cane interests, in 1898. Along with olive cultivation, which developed into one of the most dynamic sectors of Spanish agriculture before the outbreak of the Spanish Civil War, the progress of oranges and sugar beet required massive injections of capital to sustain productivity levels (Grupo de Estudios de Historia Rural, 1983; Jiménez Blanco, 1986).

This optimistic interpretation has not gone unchallenged. Antonio Miguel Bernal, for instance, emphasises the negative effects of Spain's inegalitarian structure of landed property. At one end of the scale was the *latifundio* belt of south and central Spain with its enormous unproductive estates, its absentee landlords and half-starved labouring masses. At the opposite extreme, the north and north-west of the peninsula were scattered with millions of tiny parcels of land, known as *minifundios*, incapable of supporting much more than subsistence farming. Both extremes, Bernal informs us, were archaic. Yet neither was completely stagnant and both were profitable. For their part, the great estates, which were typical of Andalusia, afforded their exploiters the availability of cheap labour together with the presence of a repressive rural police force (the *guardia civil*). The utilisation of labour-saving agricultural machinery remained largely a threat to deter hired hands from putting in excessive wage claims. Prices and profits were kept high by tariff protection, while a depreciating peseta discouraged imports. Elsewhere, the *minifundios* lacked capital and technology, yet they benefited from inexpensive labour in the shape of the extended family. Emigrant remittances from displaced members of the peasant community, moreover, permitted the redemption of leases (*foros*) and the modernisation of farms and equipment. Thus, both latifundism and minifundism stayed viable well into the twentieth century. However, the underperformance of Spanish agriculture, with its recurring crises and feudal social structures, convinced progressives of the urgent need for agrarian reform. Above all, in the case of the *latifundios* of the south, the social costs of government inertia were peasant agitation, violence and repression, which reached a climax in the brutal conflict of 1936–9 (Bernal, 1985).

Agricultural productivity in early twentieth-century Spain was pathetically low. According to Bernal, during the period 1900–30, it stood at approximately 30–40 per cent below the average of most advanced European nations. In addition, much of Spain's most fertile soils were devoted to cereal cultivation, with some of the lowest yields in Europe. As late as 1931, three quarters of the cultivated surface was dedicated to cereals and vegetables, which together generated 45 per cent of agricultural income (Bernal, 1991; Tortella, 1984).

Industrial expansion

It is a commonly-held opinion among Spanish economic historians that poor agricultural productivity, which resulted in chronically low per capita incomes among rural consumers, in turn put the brakes on industrial development. Weak demand for manufactured goods probably contributed also to the extremely conservative behaviour of Spanish entrepreneurs. Their high costs of production made Spanish goods uncompetitive in world markets.

Thrown back on an impoverished domestic market after the loss of Spain's American empire at the start of the nineteenth century, modern industry was largely confined to a few isolated pockets on the periphery. Foremost among these islands of progress were Catalonia, centre of the cotton textile industry – Spain's leading industrial sector; the Basque province of Vizcaya, with its metallurgical and shipbuilding concerns; and the coalmining region of Asturias. In partial compensation for their comparative disadvantages, Spain's industrialists, along with the country's cereal growers spearheaded the campaign for higher protective tariffs. As José Luis García Delgado shows, during the first third of the present century the Madrid authorities, whatever their political hue, found themselves under constant pressure from the millowners of Barcelona, the steelmakers of Bilbao and the Asturian mineowners for the banning of imports and the reservation of the Spanish market for domestic products. Their strident appeals for economic nationalism were rewarded by a plethora of interventionist measures, ranging from enhanced customs duties in 1906 and 1922 to grants, subsidies and direct purchases by state agencies. According to Enrique Fuentes, Spain, whose economy had been opened up by foreign trade and inward investment in the previous century, was soon converted into the most closed economy in the capitalist world (García Delgado, 1984; Fuentes Quintana, 1986).

The best indicator we have of Spain's industrial performance, Albert Carreras's index of industrial production, shows a pronounced deceleration in the process of industrialisation after 1890, which persisted until the Civil War, with the exception of the period 1922–30 (mainly coinciding with the dictatorship of General Miguel Primo de Rivera) when industrial growth attained an average of 5.5 per cent a year (Carreras, 1984). The generally pessimistic conclusions which Carreras draws from his index possibly overstate the significance of the long-time decline of Spain's mining sector, provoked by a sharp drop in external demand for iron ore, pyrites and lead. Moreover, as Jordi Maluquer argues, Carreras's essentially statistical approach fails to bring out the country's changing economic structure as well as the diversification of the industrial sector which benefited from tariff protection, the depreciation of the peseta and Spain's neutrality during the First World War (Maluquer, 1987).

In addition to the revival of artisan industries such as papermaking and publishing, the period 1900–36 saw noteworthy expansion, stimulated by technological advances, in metallurgy, shipbuilding, the manufacture of railway material, furniture and food processing. Among new industries which took off at this time were automobiles and aircraft construction. Another successful industry, cement production, which was highly energy-intensive, was a significant beneficiary of the spectacular expansion of electricity supply. The remarkable upsurge in Carreras's index in the middle and late 1920s reflects, among other factors, Spain's belated urbanisation, above all a boom in residential construction in the expanding cities of Madrid and Barcelona (Gómez Mendoza, 1986). After 1927, heavy industry, especially in Vizcaya, experienced a phase of short-lived prosperity due, in large part, to the Primo de Rivera regime's espousal of large-scale public works projects, including road building, railway construction, electrification and irrigation. In 1930, after the dictator's downfall, his infrastructural plans were abandoned because of their perceived inflationary implications, to the detriment of the real economy (Harrison, 1985).

Despite evidence of a recession in the heavy goods sector after 1930, Spain stood aloof from the worst excesses of the inter-war slump which engulfed the western world. Two of Spain's leading economic historians, Josep Fontana and Jordi Nadal, go so far as to assert that the gravest problems which confronted the ill-fated Second Republic did not result from external or conjunctural factors but from long-term structural problems, especially in agriculture. Here above all, lay the origins of most of the strains and stresses that were to explode into three years of internecine strife (Fontana and Nadal, 1976).

2
An outline of economic development since the Civil War

The Franco regime's efforts to reconstruct the Spanish economy after the Civil War turned out to be a long and painful process. Not until 1950 did the index of industrial production move above the peak year of 1929. Agricultural production only reached that level in 1958 (Carreras, 1984; García Delgado, 1987). As late as the mid 1950s, it was calculated, the average Spaniard subsisted on a daily diet of the minimum number of calories and proteins necessary for bare survival (Barciela, 1986). Albert Carreras's reworking of Spain's national income estimates for 1941–5 demonstrates an average annual increase of one per cent, which did little to make amends for an average drop of six per cent a year between 1936 and 1940. His index of industrial production shows a fall of 0.8 per cent a year between 1941 and 1945. From 1946 to 1950 the same indicator reveals a 10 per cent rise overall which compares unfavourably with increases of 70 to 110 per cent in three other countries of Mediterranean Europe: Italy, Greece and Yugoslavia (Carreras, 1984, 1989).

Official interpretations of Spain's miserable economic performance in the first decade after the Civil War usually put the blame on factors beyond the control of the Spanish authorities, not least damage caused by three years of conflict, prolonged drought (dubbed '*la pertinaz sequía*') and ostracism by the international community after 1945. Yet to most Spanish economic historians, such explanations are little more than *post hoc* excuses for failure. Destruction brought about by the Civil War, they contend, was far less than that wreaked upon the nations of central and eastern Europe during the next six years. Moreover, the main industrial sectors of Catalonia – textiles, chemicals and metallurgy – were hardly affected by the war. Even in defeat, the Basque Republican government refused to carry out a scorched earth policy. As to the so-called enduring drought, which badly restricted agricultural yields, this could easily have been alleviated by a realistic policy of irrigation along with the provision of foreign currency to purchase much-needed chemical fertilisers. Finally, such matters as the United Nations' boycott of the former ally of the Axis powers, thereby denying Franco's Spain precious amounts of economic aid, have to be seen, first and foremost, as a logical consequence of the *Caudillo*'s persistent refusal to countenance political liberalisation (Clavera *et al.*, 1978; González, 1979; Comín, 1986; García Delgado, 1986; Tortella, 1986; Catalán, 1989).

There is little dispute that the fundamental cause of the undistinguished economic record of the New Order, particularly in the first decade of its existence, was the Francoist authorities' obsession with half-baked interventionist schemes aimed at bringing about some mythical form of self-sufficiency. Major economic decisions, meanwhile, were largely entrusted to a coterie of army and naval officers and military engineers who tried to run the country like a military barracks (Tusell, 1988; Velasco, 1988). The opportunity cost of their pet projects was of little or no concern to them. Technical feasibility was the paramount criterion when it came to policy making (Velasco, 1984). Pedro Schwartz and Manuel-Jesús González characterise their attitude thus: if there is no coal beneath the ground or an unforested hillside, or an unharnessed waterfall, why not allocate resources to bring them into production (Schwartz and González, 1978).

The regime's forlorn quest for autarky led to the imposition of arbitrary bureaucratic controls down to the most trivial decision. While the dictator himself displayed a crass ignorance of elementary economic principles, the incompetence and venality of his ministers and the army of underpaid civil servants who implemented policy became legendary. Farmers and industrialists, in search of a particular commodity, often had no alternative than to bribe a corrupt administrator or turn to the black market (Fusi, 1985; Tedde, 1986; Payne, 1987).

Policies of protectionism and import substitution, already in the ascendancy before the Civil War, were massively reinforced after 1939 by an arsenal of interventionist measures and devices. While exports were thwarted by an overvalued peseta, imports of raw materials that were to be found in the peninsula, whatever their quality or costs of extraction, were generally prohibited. In addition, to tackle Spain's perennial trade deficit, the authorities resorted to a gamut of quotas and import licences (Donges, 1976; González, 1979).

By the final years of the 1940s, it was evident to all but the most blinkered ideologue of the regime that Spain's autarkic policies had failed disastrously. As bankers and foreign diplomats reported, the economy was plagued by crucial shortages of basic foodstuffs, raw materials and capital goods. The road and railway systems were in a state of near collapse. In addition, Spaniards suffered the consequences of the worst inflation in the country's recent history (Harrison, 1991). No recovery appeared remotely possible in either agricultural or industrial production without a major crash programme of imports. Yet where were the required funds to come from? Notwithstanding the frantic machinations in Washington on Spain's behalf of a well-orchestrated 'Spanish Lobby' of influential American Catholics, anti-communists, military planners and businessmen with interests in the peninsula, the country remained firmly excluded from the European Recovery Program (Marshall Aid). Fortunately for the Franco regime, between 1947 and 1949, Spain was bailed out by credits of $264 million from the sympathetic Perón regime in Argentina. Yet this sum was largely used to purchase cereals and other foodstuffs to feed a starving population. Moreover, in July 1950 Argentina, itself experiencing economic difficulties, suspended all credit sales to Spain. Then, in November 1950, as the Cold War worsened, the US Congress approved a modest loan of $62.5 million to an administration which had consistently pleaded its forthright opposition to the Red Menace. Despite objections from the Truman White House, which delayed payment, a new political climate emerged culminating in 1953 with the signing of a military and economic agreement with the Eisenhower administration (Fanjul, 1980; Viñas, 1981, 1982, 1984).

Economic growth and instability

With the provision of United States' aid, the 1950s witnessed a phase of impressive economic growth and structural change south of the Pyrenees. National income, measured at constant prices, rose by 54 per cent over the decade, while the proportion of the active labour force employed on the land dropped from 49.9 per cent in 1950 to 42.5 per cent in 1959. Carreras's index of industrial production shows a yearly increase of 6.6 per cent in the period 1951–5 and 7.4 per cent between 1956 and 1960, despite the deflationary impact of the Stabilisation Plan of 1959. However, industrial expansion was not achieved without a sharp rise in the level of inflation after 1954 and severe balance-of-payments problems from 1956 onwards (Carreras, 1984; García Delgado, 1987).

The marked upturn in Spain's economic fortunes after 1951, precarious though it was, coincided with the *Caudillo*'s decision in July of that year to reshape his cabinet. In particular, the new Minister of Commerce, Manuel Arburúa, tried to facilitate an increase in specific types of imports. In an endeavour to stabilise food prices and eliminate the most glaring aspects of the black market in the countryside, the new minister permitted a significant increase in the price of foodstuffs. He also set out to eliminate a variety of problems, including low agricultural yields, bottlenecks to industrial production, energy shortages and communications problems, through imports of raw materials and capital goods. Later, after 1955, Spain experienced a pronounced increase in imports of semi-manufactures, clear evidence of previous improvements in the secondary sector. Yet despite hopes among economic liberals that he would open up the Spanish economy to outside competition, Arburúa remained firmly tied to the goal of import substitution. As a result, Spain's industrialisation policy continued to be underpinned by an assortment of protectionist measures, multiple exchange rates, and so on (Donges, 1976; Clavera *et al.*, 1978; Braña *et al.*, 1979; González, 1979; Viñas *et al.*, 1979).

In the short- and medium-term, the country's inability to generate a significant increase in export earnings to finance the necessary imports only served to emphasise the importance to the economy of American aid, especially during the middle years of the decade. Between 1951 and 1957, the United States furnished Spain with $625 million of aid. It is generally accepted that America's generosity, while small by Marshall Aid standards, offered a vital breathing space to the Franco regime which might otherwise have succumbed. Above all, it offset part of the current account shortfall and was a key factor in combating inflation and securing higher living standards (González, 1979; Viñas *et al.*, 1979).

Even so, by the winter of 1956–7, when US aid began to run out, Arburúa's timid attempts to liberalise the Spanish economy were in disarray. In December 1956, as inflation mounted, rumours circulated that Spain's gold reserves had fallen as low as $40 million. Faced with the prospect of national bankruptcy, the discredited minister recommended a package of severe austerity measures. Two months later, Franco sacked him in a cabinet reshuffle which brought to prominence a new breed of technocrats, hitherto politically inexperienced, closely associated with the Catholic lay group, *Opus Dei*. Alberto Ullastres, a 43-year-old university professor, replaced Arburúa at the Ministry of Commerce, while the Finance portfolio went to Mariano Navarro Rubio, a lawyer and economist of the same age. They joined forces with another member of their association, Laureano López Rodó, already appointed Technical Secretary of the Presidency in December 1956 (Payne, 1987). The new team was to be ably assisted by a distinguished group of economists, among them Juan Sardà at the Bank of Spain, Juan Antonio García Ortiz at Finance and Manuel Varela at Commerce (Fuentes Quintana, 1984). Together they embarked, hesitantly at first, along the obstacle-strewn path from autarky to the introduction of market mechanisms. Yet, as Eduardo Merigó informs us, economic liberalisation was not to be equated with the introduction of greater political freedoms (Merigó, 1982).

Over the next two years before the presentation of the Stabilisation Plan in July 1959, the technocrats pursued a series of cautious initiatives though, in the opinion of Manuel-Jesús González, it is hard to discern any deliberate line of policy (González, 1979). In April 1957, the system of multiple exchange rates was simplified and the peseta devalued, though by not enough. Moreover, the plethora of economic controls was retained and, in some cases, extended. Perhaps the most significant development of this period, sometimes dubbed pre-stabilisation, was that Spain became a member of a number of international institutions which were later to underwrite the 1959 Plan. In January 1958, she joined the

Organisation for European Economic Cooperation (OEEC), soon
to become the Organisation for Economic Cooperation and Development (OECD). Six months later, Spain became a member of
the International Monetary Fund and the World Bank. These
bodies provided the Spanish authorities with invaluable technical
assistance and facilitated the acceptance of new ideas and methods
(Viñas *et al.*, 1979; Muns, 1986; Navarro Rubio, 1991).

Stabilisation and development

The so-called Stabilisation and Liberalisation Plan of 1959 was
unveiled against a background of near insolvency. Spain's balance
of payments, in almost permanent crisis since 1957, gave rise to
extraordinary concern during the first half of 1959 when the Bank
of Spain's gold and foreign currency reserves, net of short-term
liabilities, presented a negative figure (Merigó, 1982). The Plan,
which was dispatched to the International Monetary Fund and the
OEEC as memorandum, had two main objectives. Internally, it
aimed to restore financial stability by enacting a series of monetary
and fiscal measures designed to restrict demand and limit inflation.
Additionally, the Plan declared the government's intention to
liberalise foreign trade and promote inward investment (Sardà,
1970).

In order to bring down domestic inflation, the authorities
imposed drastic reductions in public sector borrowing. Direct
advances by the Bank of Spain to public institutions were cut from
11 billion pesetas in 1958 to 3.4 billions in 1959. Meanwhile, in an
attempt to balance the budget for the public sector, the government announced price increases of up to 50 per cent for transport
and public utilities. Taxes on tobacco and petroleum, both state
monopolies, were also put up. In the short-run, more serious
damage to business activity ensued from the raising of the central
bank's rediscount rate from 5 to 6.5 per cent. This had negative
repercussions throughout the financial system. However, the most
far-reaching measures dealt with Spain's foreign trade and
payment system. Multiple exchange rates were abolished and the
peseta fixed at a par of 60 to the US dollar. Quotas and other
restrictions were removed from about half of Spanish imports from

OECD countries. In addition, legislation was brought forward which offered enticing guarantees and incentives to foreign investors. Among other undertakings, proposed or implied in the Plan, were a long-overdue revision of the country's outdated tariff legislation, measures against restrictive practices, a reform of Spain's inadequate and regressive taxation system and the initiation of long-range economic planning. Although all of these proposals passed into law, as Charles Anderson maintains, three at least were to prove a disappointment to economic liberals. The new tariff of 1960 was still strongly protectionist. Not until 1963 was a toothless anti-monopoly law enacted while the tax reforms proposed in 1959 did not come into operation until five years later (Anderson, 1970; Gonzàlez, 1979).

Many commentators consider the monetary and fiscal policies brought in during the second half of 1959 as far too harsh. That they did not provoke a severe recession was mainly due to unplanned-for developments, not least the start of mass tourism (Rubio Jiménez, 1968; Poveda, 1980; Varela, 1989–90). In the long-run, however, the Stabilisation Plan of 1959, unlike the planning mechanism of 1964–75 discussed below, gave a positive stimulus to economic activity which brought Spain closer to the market system and began to expose domestic producers to outside competition (González, 1979; Ros Hombravella, 1979; Fuentes Quintana, 1984).

In the decade and a half after the introduction of the Stabilisation Plan, Spain experienced unprecedented economic growth. The country's GDP, at constant prices, grew by 7.2 per cent per annum between 1960 and 1973, compared with the OECD average of 5 per cent. Only Japan boasted faster and more sustained growth rates. Even so, as Enrique Fuentes and Jaime Requeijo stress, this growth was far from evenly distributed throughout the economy. While industrial production at this time expended by an annual rate of 10.2 per cent, the service sector grew by 6.7 per cent and agriculture by no more than 2.3 per cent a year (Fuentes Quintana and Requeijo, 1984).

If the authoritarian regime of General Franco sought to provide a certain degree of legitimacy for its continued existence by claiming responsibility for what propagandists termed Spain's 'economic miracle', critics tended to highlight structural problems created by rapid and unbalanced growth. They also maintained, with justification, that Spain was only able to finance the massive rise in imports of foodstuffs, raw materials, semi-manufactures and capital goods which made possible the high growth rates because of three largely exogenous variables: a massive increase in the earnings from foreign tourism, emigrant remittances from over one million Spaniards forced to seek work abroad, and a renewal of foreign investment in the Spanish economy (Anderson, 1970; Fuentes Quintana and Requeijo, 1984; Estapé and Amado, 1986).

Other factors too played a part in Spain's spectacular upsurge. Economists emphasise the presence in the Spanish countryside of a vast reserve of underemployed labour. While, on the land, the marginal productivity of these workers was close to zero, they constituted a source of cheap and abundant labour for the industrial and service sectors. Entrepreneurs were thereby spared the cost of inflationary wage agreements as they increased the size of their work force (Martínez Serrano *et al.*, 1982). Additionally, and of great significance in the long-run, Spain's high rate of industrial growth and rising living standards in the 1960s and early 1970s was made possible by the availability of plentiful supplies of low-cost energy, especially imported oil. Many of Spain's most rapidly-expanding industries, such as metallurgy, shipbuilding and cement, were energy intensive. In 1961, 29.8 per cent of the country's energy came from oil. By 1974, and the beginning of the first oil crisis, provoked by OPEC's decision to quadruple the price of oil, that figure had jumped to 67.8 per cent (Fuentes Quintana and Requeijo, 1984).

The planners in power, 1964–75

After Spain's adherence to the planning mechanism in 1962, and the appointment of López Rodó as Commissioner of the Plan, a new ruling elite, representing big business and financial interests, gained a firm hold on the reins of economic policy. Writers such as Manuel-Jesús González contend that a second generation of technocrats, led by López Rodó and new Industry Minister Gregorio López Bravo, deliberately watered down the liberalising achievements of the Stabilisation Plan. Ignoring the recommendations of the World Bank and the OECD, the so-called Men of Development set out to gain additional discretionary power for themselves. Moreover, most economists now agree that, had Spain persevered with the policies of economic liberalisation and exposure to market forces, the country would have secured not only faster growth but also lower inflation and greater economic efficiency (González, 1979; Fuentes Quintana and Requeijo, 1984; Martí, 1989–90).

Indeed, as Ramón Tamames argues, the Spanish system of planning which came into operation in 1964 was a poor imitation of France's indicative planning introduced in 1946. Tamames, one of the Franco's regime's most vehement critics, maintains that scant consideration was given as to how well the French model suited the structural problems of the Spanish economy nor whether Spain's entrepreneurs were likely to react in the same way as their northern counterparts to the stimuli provided by the planners (Tamames, 1989–90).

In essence, the public sector was compelled to meet targets set by the planners, while the authorities tried to direct the activities of the private sector through a range of indirect methods. These included credit and fiscal measures, as well as a process known as concerted action, involving agreements between individual firms and the relevant ministry aimed at securing an agreed level of output (González, 1979).

Three plans were implemented during the period 1964–75. Their main objectives, as summarised by Rosa Alsina, were economic development, the promotion of a market economy, greater integration into the international system and lastly (and of least importance to the planners) improvements in social welfare. All three plans (1964–7, 1968–71, 1972–5) aimed at securing large increases in production and encouraged investment at the expense of consumption. Hence, industry was assigned higher priority than agriculture. Apart from the second plan, inflation and a deteriorating trade balance were deemed a necessary price to be paid for fast growth. Overall, the planners' stop-go policies brought a six per cent annual increase in GDP, at current prices, between 1964–75. However, none of the Planning Commission's predictions were borne out by later developments while, after 1973, the destabilising effects of the world crisis blew the third plan well off course (Alsina, 1987).

How far was Spain's economic expansion at this time a product of the planning experience? If we bear in mind the favourable international circumstances before 1973, it seems likely that the country's economy would have prospered come what may. The regime's detractors are quick to point out that higher growth rates were attained in the triennium 1961–3, before the planners could claim credit for any achievement (González, 1979; Ros Hombravella, 1979). In a recent survey article, the distinguished economist and former deputy prime minister, Enrique Fuentes, charges the Men of Development with bringing about *unbalanced* growth and closing down the opportunities for expansion during the second half of the 1960s (Fuentes Quintana, 1988).

Crisis and readjustment

After 1971, the Spanish authorities were presented with disturbing signs of rising inflation and a widening trade gap. Even so, nothing prepared them for the sequence of economic shocks which beset the country in the second half of the 1970s. In common with other industrial powers, Spain felt the full force of the dramatic increase in the price of raw materials and foodstuffs which occurred in 1973–4. Above all, in 1974, the nation's bill for imported oil and other sources of energy more than trebled, from 72.9 billion pesetas to 225.8 billions. The share of energy in total imports soared from 13 per cent in 1973 to an average of 27.4 per cent in the period 1974–8. After a second oil crisis in 1979, brought on by events in Iran, the cost of imported oil reached alarming proportions. Spain, with its weak energy base, spent 1,259 billion pesetas on these items in 1981, 42.4 per cent of the total import bill (García Alonso, 1983).

These difficulties, serious as they were, were exacerbated by a second set of problems resulting from changes in the structure of international trade which favoured the so-called Newly-Industrialising Countries (NICs), such as Mexico, Brazil and the Far East, where labour costs were below Spanish levels. As a result, Spanish producers faced cut-throat competition in textiles, footwear, electrical goods, iron and steel, shipbuilding, and so on. This challenge was to have a considerable effect on employment prospects in the long term. To maintain full employment, a substantial reduction in real wages was required (Rojo, 1987).

Spain's economic misfortunes, which gave cause for concern until the mid 1980s, are clearly illustrated by the leading indicators. Over the period 1975–83, GDP, at constant prices, rose by no more than 1.6 per cent per annum, less than one third of the rate achieved in the previous decade. During the same period, the level of inflation escalated to an average of 16.8 per cent. At the end of 1983, 18.1 per cent of the working population was registered as unemployed (Fuentes Quintana and Requeijo, 1984).

It was Spain's bad luck that the post-1973 crisis hit the country as it embarked on the lengthy process of political transition from dictatorship to democracy. Fears of military rebellion or working-class unrest meant that pressing economic issues were relegated to a secondary position. Economic ministers complained that their capacity to take remedial action was effectively constrained by overriding political considerations. Above all, after the death of Franco in November 1975 down to the first free elections in June 1977, Spain lived through a high degree of political uncertainty which gave rise to timid and occasionally irresponsible government. Luis Angel Rojo, head of research at the Bank of Spain, recounts how the early stages of the crisis saw the accumulation of a series of problems, both internal and external in origin, in the face of which the Spanish authorities lacked a strategy for containment, let alone one for confronting the deteriorating situation. On the eve of the polls in 1977, Spain's annual inflation rate stood at 26 per cent. Over the previous twelve months, hourly wages in the manufacturing sector had risen 30 per cent before tax, completely wiping out the beneficial effects of 20 per cent devaluation of the peseta in February 1976 (Rojo, 1987).

Finally, in October 1977, the newly-elected centre-right administration of Adolfo Suárez, in the midst of an agitated social climate, decided to face up to the reality of the situation and tackle Spain's multifarious economic problems via a policy of political consensus. Accordingly, the government signed an agreement, known as the Moncloa Pacts, with the opposition Socialist and Communist parties. To curb the runaway inflation, a 22 per cent wage ceiling was imposed which, it was hoped, the recently-legalised trade union movement would accept in return for important institutional and economic reforms. As its part of the bargain, the government affirmed its intention of bringing down the level of inflation to 15 per cent by the end of 1978, a target which it only narrowly missed. In their determination to head off social and political turmoil, the nation's leaders undoubtedly permitted real wages to rise far too quickly relative to productivity increases. The upshot of their gradualist strategy was a sharp increase in the jobless total. Moreover, any advance in Spain's economic performance in the wake of the Moncloa accord was soon swept aside by the second wave of oil price increases in 1979 (Fuentes Quintana and Requeijo, 1984).

The next three years brought few promising signs. As employers struggled to hold down wage costs, unemployment passed two million, in percentage terms the highest rate in Europe. Felipe González's Socialists came to power in October 1982 pledged to create an additional 800,000 jobs. Yet once in office, the Socialist administration abandoned this commitment, partly due to the bad experiences of the Mitterrand administration in trying to reinflate the French economy in isolation. Under Finance Ministers Miguel Boyer and Carlos Solchaga, Spain speeded up the process of gradual readjustment initiated by Suárez in 1977. The main pillars of the Socialists' economic programme south of the Pyrenees were sound finance, bringing down inflation, control of public expenditure and industrial restructuring.

Unemployment aside, which remained stubbornly high, the González government could claim a moderate degree of success in its implementation of what Fuentes and Requeijo term 'the inevitable economic policy' (Fuentes Quintana and Requeijo, 1984). During their first term in office, the Socialists halved the rate of inflation, while growth rates began to climb, if not spectacularly. Spain's GDP, at constant prices, rose steadily from 1.4 per cent in 1982 to 3 per cent in 1986. From 1987 to 1989, despite the government's inability to maintain social harmony with the trade unions, Spain once more began to enjoy respectable economic growth as GDP increased by 5.3 per cent per annum. Over the same period, inflation was kept below seven per cent, yet Spain's balance of trade deteriorated sharply. In 1989, imports exceeded exports by $24.3 billion. Moreover, this shortfall was only partly offset by a surplus on the services account of $12.1 billions (Banco Bilbao Vizcaya, 1990).

On 1 January 1986, towards the end of the Socialists' first term in office, Spain became a full member of the European Community, twenty-four years after the Franco regime petitioned for membership. The conditions of entry were harsh. Spain's negotiators committed the country to opening her market to EC competitors and to bringing down her external tariff on industrial goods from third countries to the Community average within a period of seven years. In return, it would take ten years for the most competitive sectors of Spanish farming (fresh fruit, vegetables and olive oil) to be phased into the Common Agricultural Policy. Moreover, EC rights on the free movement of labour between member states were withheld from Spaniards for a period of seven years.

3
Demographic developments

During the first eight decades of the present century, the number of Spaniards doubled, from 18.6 million persons in 1900 to 37.6 millions according to the 1981 census. In other words, the net annual population expansion over this period was 0.88 per cent. Only during the 1920s, and again in the 1960s, did the average expansion for an entire decade exceed one per cent a year. Although this experience hardly constitutes a population explosion, Spanish demographers tend to speak of a demographic revolution. As Joaquín Arango argues, since at no stage in Spain's previous history had the population grown by more than 0.5 per cent annually for any length of time, the twentieth century presents us with a pronounced discontinuity in the long-term trend (Arango, 1987).

Evidence of a demographic revolution is furnished by a sharp fall in both the birth rate and the death rate throughout the twentieth century, shown in Table 1. The same source also testifies to two important short-lived developments against the prevailing tendency: the large number of deaths which resulted from the Spanish Civil War of 1936–9 and the upturn in the birth rate during the late 1960s and early 1970s, produced by Spain's belated 'baby boom'. In addition, as Table 1 illustrates, the demise of the ultra conservative Franco regime and the appearance of a new morality associated with the resulting democracy, led to a dramatic decline in nuptiality.

Census data reveals that during the period 1900–80, the life expectancy of Spaniards more than doubled. The average male, who survived to his thirty-fourth birthday in 1900, lived on to 47 years in 1940 and 71 in 1982. Among females, the average life expectancy went up from 36 years in 1900, to 53 in 1940 and 78 in 1982. Thus, especially after the middle of the century, Spain witnessed a gradual ageing of its inhabitants. The proportion of Spaniards over 65 years of age increased from 5.2 per cent in 1900, to 6.1 per cent in 1930, 7.2 per cent in 1950, 9.7 per cent in 1970 and 11.3 per cent in 1981. In certain rural provinces, where there was a strong tendency among the younger generation to migrate to the cities, the proportion of senior citizens within the total population was much higher. For example, in 1981 it stood at 18.5 per cent in Soria, 18.2 per cent in Lugo, 17.7 per cent in Teruel and 17.5 per cent in Zamora (Nicolau, 1989; Tezanos, 1989).

In terms of density, Spain remained relatively underpopulated by European standards. As the number of inhabitants doubled between 1900 and 1981, population density per square kilometre rose from 36.8 to 74.6. The latter figure contrasted with 98 persons in France, 189 in Italy, 323 in Belgium and 345 in the Netherlands. Within the peninsula, enormous disparities existed between predominantly industrial and agricultural zones. In 1981, for example, the province of Barcelona supported 597 inhabitants per square kilometre, Madrid 591 and Vizcaya 532. At the opposite end of the scale, Soria registered only nine persons, Teruel 10, Guadalajara and Cuenca 12 (Tezanos, 1989).

The post Civil War period

Estimates vary as to the extent of deaths caused by the Spanish Civil War. Hugh Thomas puts the number of persons killed in battle or who died later from their wounds at slightly more than 200,000 – one-tenth of all combatants. A further 130,000 murders and executions took place behind the lines, while there were 10,000 deaths from air raids and 25,000 from malnutrition and disease arising from the conflict. In addition, 100,000 Republicans perished as a result of post-war reprisals, bringing the total sum of victims to approximately half a million. Furthermore, among defeated Republicans who went into exile during the first months of 1939, 300,000 preferred permanent emigration rather than risk victimisation in Franco's New Order (Thomas, 1977).

A more imaginative approach to the practically impossible task

Table 1 *Marriages, births and deaths, 1900–86 (per thousand inhabitants)*

Year	Marriages	Births	Deaths	Net growth
1900	8.67	33.76	28.86	4.90
1910	7.02	32.58	22.97	9.61
1920	8.27	29.36	23.29	6.07
1930	7.42	28.19	16.83	11.36
1940	8.38	24.37	16.50	7.87
1950	7.50	20.06	10.80	9.26
1960	7.79	21.60	8.65	12.95
1970	7.36	19.50	8.33	11.17
1980	5.71	15.12	7.69	7.43
1986	5.26	11.24	7.93	3.31

Source: Tezanos, 1989.

of calculating the extent of fatalities was attempted by the Spanish demographer Juan Díez Nicolás. The latter compares the number of deaths recorded during the civil-war period with those which might have been expected to take place if previous trends in mortality had persisted. Díez Nicolás's calculations lead him to conclude that an excess of 344,000 deaths occurred during the three years of the conflict, together with a further 214,000 in the period 1940–2. This leaves us with a total of 558,000 fatalities either directly attributable to the Civil War or to hunger, malnutrition, substandard living conditions and post-war repression. After 1943, he argues, the pre-civil war tendency in mortality was resumed (Díez Nicolás, 1985b; Arango, 1987).

With regard to the birth rate, Díez Nicolás explains that the high figure recorded in 1940 of 24.37 births per thousand inhabitants (see Table 1) was largely the product of late registration due to problems faced by parents in reporting the birth of an offspring in the course of the conflict (Díez Nicolás, 1971). Thereafter, Arango refers to a 'quasi stabilisation' of the birth rate during the period 1943–64 at a lower magnitude than before the Civil War. The subsequent minor baby boom, between 1965 and 1976, occurred at a time when the rest of Europe was experiencing a marked drop in fecundity. One explanation of this phenomenon is that modern forms of birth control, such as the contraceptive pill, readily available north of the Pyrenees, were still illegal in Franco's Spain. For the Spanish authorities, the sharp acceleration in the birthrate of the late 1960s and first half of the 1970s was to create a variety of problems in the long-run, not least in the provision of all forms of education and in the size of the labour force (Díez Nicolás, 1985a; Arango, 1987).

Concerning the distribution of Spain's working population since the Civil War, the most significant feature was the drastic fall in both the relative and absolute size of the agricultural sector. Between 1940 and 1981, agriculture and fisheries declined from supporting 50.5 per cent of the active population to 13.9 per cent. During the 'fifties and 'sixties, according to Roser Nicolau, 2.3 million men abandoned the countryside, more than one-half of the male labour force (Nicolau, 1989). In 1965, the factory overtook the farm as the leading employer of labour. From the end of the 1970s, however, the proportion of the working population engaged in manufacturing industry began to fall, as the service sector went on to account for the majority of Spaniards in registered employment.

Population movements

After disruption caused by the Second World War, emigration was resumed on a small-scale after 1945, mostly towards Latin America. Nicolau estimates that between 1947 and 1962 an average of 44,000 persons a year set sail in that direction, mainly to Venezuela. Fifty per cent of all emigrants originated from Galicia, 13 per cent from the Canary Islands, 9 per cent from Cantabria and 9 per cent from Catalonia (Nicolau, 1989).

From the beginning of the 1960s, however, there was a radical change in the destination of Spaniards seeking work abroad. The major 'pull' factor was the sustained economic expansion of the developed nations of Western Europe which generated a strong and continuous demand for unskilled labour in the industrial and service sectors. In geographical terms, France absorbed over half the flow of 'guest workers' from Spain, followed by West Germany, Belgium and Switzerland. Within Spain, it was the regions of surplus agricultural labour, above all Andalusia, Galicia and Extremadura, which provided most of the outflow. According to official statistics, 2.34 million Spaniards departed the fatherland between 1960 and 1973 in search of a better job, half of them looking for temporary work, half permanent employment. Yet Spanish demographers are convinced that government figures understate the extent of emigration. Nicolau, basing her calculations on data derived from the official statistics of the countries of destination, puts the number of Spaniards emigrating between 1960 and 1967 at 1.88 million, with a further 1.21 million leaving between 1968 and 1973 (Nicolau, 1989). After the oil crisis of the late 1970s put paid to the heady expansion of the European economies, the current of Spaniards moving northwards slowed down considerably and was later reversed. Between 1976 and 1981, Spain experienced a net immigration of 270,000 persons (Tezanos, 1989).

During the 1960s and early 1970s, emigration acted as an important safety valve against the dangers of unemployment. Emigrant remittances also made a contribution to Spain's balance of payments. Yet, in a strictly demographic sense, internal migration was a more significant phenomenon at this time. The transformation of Spain from an agricultural to a modern industrial and service economy led to a massive exodus of rural workers from Andalusia, Extremadura, Galicia, the two Castiles and Murcia. Over the same period, Catalonia, Madrid, Valencia and the Basque Country were the main areas of immigration. After 1976, this pattern altered lightly. While Extremadura and the two Castiles continued to export surplus population, Andalusia and Galicia broke even and Murcia was converted into a net recipient. Among the country's more developed regions, only Madrid and Valencia grew in size in the late 1970s. In contrast, the Basque Country, whose basic industries were plunged into crisis, lost population after 1976, while Catalonia became a net exporter after 1981 (Tezanos, 1989).

Internal migration from the countryside to the cities brought with it delayed urbanisation. In 1940, 51.2 per cent of Spaniards lived in towns of less than 10,000 inhabitants, while only 19.1 per cent of the population lived in large cities with over 100,000 residents. Forty years later these figures were more or less reversed. Official statistics for 1981 demonstrate that no more than 26.8 per cent of the Spanish population lived in towns below 10,000 in size while cities with over 100,000 people accounted for 42 per cent of the population. By José Félix Tezano's calculations, the number of cities with more than 100,000 inhabitants went up from 18 in 1940, to 24 in 1950, 38 in 1970 and 50 in 1981. At the end of the 1980s, six conurbations (Madrid, Barcelona, Valencia, Seville, Saragossa and Málaga) boasted a population of half a million and above, together housing almost one-fifth of the entire population (Tezanos, 1989).

4
Agriculture

A decade of depression

At the cessation of hostilities in 1939, Spanish agriculture displayed few signs of the problems which were to beset it during the next decade. Several of the more prosperous farming regions, which had comprised part of the Nationalist zone, were either untouched by the conflict or sustained little damage. In Republican areas, agricultural production had shown surprising vitality. Wartime destruction of crops, animals, farm buildings and agricultural machinery was slight. Only in the cases of mules and oxen could temporary shortages be said to exist (Tió, 1982; Barciela, 1986). Yet, throughout the 1940s, the Spanish countryside was engulfed in a profound crisis.

For their part, the Francoist authorities tried to explain away declining yields and widespread hunger in terms of the damage cause by the Reds (thereby implying that the rebel army had waged war selectively), the ubiquitous 'enduring drought', a lack of resources to import tractors and chemical fertilisers and the activities of the *maquis*. Yet, as Carlos Barciela contends, the New State was partly to blame for its own adversities. Above all, he lampoons the regime's flawed interventionist ideology which naïvely asserted that such matters as levels of output, wages and prices could be preordained by the promulgation of decrees. Market forces were deemed to be of minor significance (Naredo, 1974; Barciela, 1986).

The regime's abiding passion for self-sufficiency in foodstuffs led to a specialisation in basic staples. In particular, interventionist schemes set out to stimulate the production of wheat and olive oil. Precious little was done to encourage the expansion of export crops like citrus fruits where Spain was known to enjoy a comparative advantage in world trade. A decree of December 1942 imposed an upper limit on the planting of orange trees (López de Sebastián, 1970). Yet the most lamentable manifestation of state interference on the land was the National Wheat Service (*Servicio Nacional del Trigo*). Established in August 1937, in the throes of the Civil War, the SNT was charged with guaranteeing wheat prices along with purchasing, storing and disposing of the entire harvest. Its impossible brief was to safeguard the livelihoods of the nation's wheat growers, a bulwark of the Franco regime, while at the same time holding down the price of bread. Not surprisingly, growers reacted to the low prices fixed for wheat by switching to more profitable crops not subject to controls. The profit motive also persuaded farmers to divert large quantities of wheat to the black market, known as the *estraperlo*. As Barciela recounts, despite the legal threat of fines and gaol sentences, the clandestine market for wheat grew even larger than the official market (Barciela, 1981). Black marketeering became a lucrative business. In his study of large estates in southern Spain, José Manuel Naredo shows that farmers who sold off part or all of their harvest on the *estraperlo* earned up to three or four times the amount they would have received from government agencies. Above all, it was the large and medium-sized landowners, who cultivated their own estates, that profited most from the interventionist system. As well as enjoying political immunity in many cases, they were usually better placed than small farmers to accumulate large surpluses and to conceal them from the authorities. In addition, large landowners were more likely to possess means of transport as well as the resources to bribe prying civil guards or over-zealous magistrates. Naredo also shows that the considerable profits from black-market operations constituted the prime source of capital for industrial investment in Spain during the late 1940s and early 1950s (Naredo, 1974, 1981, 1986).

From a 'Golden Age' to the crisis of traditional agriculture

Franco's appointment of the less dogmatic personality of Rafael Cavestany to the agriculture portfolio in July 1951 heralded a refreshing change at that ministry, hitherto renowned for its rhetorical statements rather than any specific achievements. Cavestany, Barciela informs us, had earlier rebuked the regime for its counterproductive interventionist policies. Judging these to be the main cause of Spain's perennial food shortages, the new minister permitted agricultural prices to rise in an attempt to return the country to market conditions. Cavestany also championed a handful of modest initiatives directed towards the modernisation of the primary sector. In addition, his colleague Manuel Arburúa's willingness to allocate additional amounts of foreign currency to import such items as farm machinery, artificial fertilisers and improved strains of seed contributed to a steady increase in farm output. That said, we must bear in mind that pre-civil war levels of agricultural production were not attained until the end of the 1950s. In addition, Barciela charges Cavestany, and his successor, Cirilo Cánovas, with shortsightedness with respect to the utilisation of the land surface. Even after the eradication of shortages of basic foodstuffs, the Agricultural Ministry persisted with its policy of offering costly and irrelevant subsidies to cereal farmers, viticultors and rice growers. No account whatsoever was taken of changing dietary habits among domestic consumers. Hence, livestock and dairy farming were virtually neglected by Spain's policy makers (Barciela, 1986).

Among the genuine successes of the Franco regime in the 1950s were an increase of one-third in the area of irrigated land, with consequent improvements in productivity, and a scheme known as *concentración parcelaria* aimed at the consolidation of scattered holdings in the *minifundio* belt. This measure affected 240,000 hectares of land during the decade though, as Barciela argues, its impact was restricted by the conservatism of Spanish property laws which ensured that, even after restructuring, new holdings were in general too small for significant economies of scale to be obtained by farmers. On the thorny topic of the *latifundios*, Barciela defends the minister against his more vociferous critics, by maintaining that he pursued a realistic policy which sensibly limited its horizons to cajoling large landowners, whether absent or not from their estates, into carrying out improvements in land use under the threat of expropriation by the state (Barciela, 1986).

To contemporaries, it appeared that traditional agriculture south of the Pyrenees entered a Golden Age at the end of the 1950s. Large landowners, especially those cultivating cereals on their estates, fared particularly well. Despite the beginnings of a wave of migration among farm labourers from the countryside to the big cities, labour remained a cheap and abundant factor of production. While the black market, a previous source of remunerative profits, diminished in size, food prices followed an upward trend. The Spanish population, long accustomed to privation and an empty stomach, gratefully consumed all that the nation's farmers could provide, no matter how inferior its quality. Moreover, the state continued to buy up mounting surpluses of wheat and rice. Although apparently stable, this providential situation could not persist indefinitely. It was not long before Spanish agronomists warned the authorities of the consolidation of what they termed 'the crisis of traditional agriculture' (Naredo, 1974; Leal *et al.*, 1975).

The modernisation of Spanish farming

As we have seen, from the late 1950s onwards, Spain embarked on the rapid transformation from an agrarian to an industrial society. Agriculture's contribution to GDP shrank from 18.4 per cent in 1965 to 6.1 per cent in 1981. In the intervening period, Spanish farmers, who had previously been largely cushioned against the deleterious effects of change by government policy, faced two main threats to their traditional ways of life. These challenges were posed by escalating production costs and a contraction in domestic demand for many of their products (García Delgado and Muñoz Cidad, 1988).

In terms of their costs of production, the most pressing issue was rising wages. García Delgado and Muñoz Cidad estimate that between 1964 and 1976, agricultural wages shot up by 450 per cent, while the cost of other inputs (fuel, fertilisers, seeds, fodder, etc.) rose by 107 per cent. After the beginning of the energy crisis in the mid 1970s, the gap between these two indicators narrowed. From 1976 to 1984, wages paid out by farmers increased by 242 per cent while other costs rose by 212 per cent (García Delgado and Muñoz Cidad, 1988).

Table 2 *The mechanisation of farms according to size of holdings,*
1962–82

Year of census	Percentage of all tractors on holdings of under/over 100 hectares		Percentage of surface area farmed on holdings of under/over 100 hectares		No. of hectares worked per tractor on holdings of under/over 100 hectares	
1962	63.3	36.7	73.2	26.8	270	186
1972	80.0	19.8	67.0	33.0	56	112
1982	87.4	12.6	67.7	32.3	26	86

Source: Naredo, 1988.

In situations where economies of scale were thought to be practicable, farmers endeavoured to hold down wage costs by substituting capital for labour. Naredo demonstrates that, during the 1960s, the mechanisation of production could be highly advantageous to farmers. For example, in the case of winter-sown wheat, the purchase of a combine harvester led on average to a reduction in the number of hours spent gathering the harvest from between 100–130 hours per hectare to no more than 3–3.5 hours (Naredo, 1974).

The spread of mechanisation was one of the most outstanding features of Spanish agriculture since the 1960s. The number of tractors in operation, for example, increased from 53,000 in 1960, to 130,000 in 1964, 295,000 in 1972 and 611,000 in 1984. While initially it was the nation's large landowners who possessed the necessary finances to profit from the economies of scale which could be obtained from the use of labour-saving machinery, Naredo shows that during the 1960s, small farmers too benefited from mechanisation. Using census material, he calculates that between 1962 and 1982 the proportion of tractors in operation on holdings under one hundred hectares in size rose from 63 to 87 per cent. Even so, Naredo argues that throughout the period tractors were utilised far less efficiently on small farms than on large estates (see Table 2) (Naredo, 1988).

Deprived of adequate funds to modernise and reequip their holdings, many small farmers in northern Spain faced the stark choice of bankruptcy or going into debt with the banks. Tens of thousands of peasant families attempted to supplement their incomes by sending one or more of the household to earn an extra wage in the big conurbations or north of the frontier. Part-time farming became a distinctive feature of many villages. Many unprofitable or marginal farms were put on the market. According to the Agrarian Census, between 1962 and 1982, 560,000 farms disappeared, about one-fifth of all holdings. As a result of the concentration of holdings, the average size of farms in Spain increased from 15.6 to 18.9 hectares over the two decades. During the 1960s, when the practice of abandoning the land was at its height, over one-quarter of all holdings disappeared in León and Old Castile, a region where family farms devoted to cereal growing were common (Naredo, 1974, 1988; San Juan Mesonada and Romo Lagunas, 1987).

The second major challenge confronting Spanish farmers was the urgent requirement to match their supply of products to changes in public demand. Improvements in dietary habits, brought about by higher real incomes, led to the accumulation of vast stockpiles of unwanted wheat and rice. At the same time, Spain faced a massive import bill for dairy products and fodder crops for livestock. According to Naredo, Spain recorded a trade deficit in agricultural products of 6.4 billion pesetas in 1970, rising to 76.8 billions in 1975, then slipping to 50.8 billion pesetas in 1980. Not until 1985, when the country was on the threshold of EC membership, did exports of agricultural products overtake imports. The process of adaption to changing tastes proved slow and expensive. In particular, agronomists reproached successive administrations with squandering large quantities of taxpayers' money subsidising inefficient cereal growers (Bardají *et al.*, 1982; Pérez Blanco, 1983; Sumpsi, 1983; Barceló, 1987; Naredo, 1988).

Even so, Spanish farming made commendable advances since the 1960s. García Delgado and Muñoz Cidad calculate that agricultural output doubled between 1964 and 1984. Arable production rose by 78 per cent over the two decades, while livestock production rose by 137 per cent in real terms. Moreover, this increase occurred against the background of an unprecedented contraction in the size of the agricultural workforce. The same authors estimate that in 1984 each Spaniard employed on the land produced sufficient food to satisfy the dietary needs of twenty individuals, as against 7.5 people twenty years earlier. Furthermore, Spanish agriculture also developed a thriving exporting sector. Above all, horticultural producers on the south-east littoral and in the Canary Islands created a dynamic sector capable of holding its own in highly competitive international markets (García Delgado and Muñoz Cidad, 1988).

Nevertheless, Spain still has a long way to go in order to catch up with its rivals. France, for example, boasts a level of agricultural productivity more than twice that of neighbouring Spain. South of the Pyrenees, the average farm is far too small, while Spanish holdings remain notoriously undercapitalised. In the long-term, however, in those areas where Spain enjoys a comparative advantage in world trade, such as horticulture, her farmers can be expected to reap rich rewards.

5
Industry

Without doubt, the most outstanding aspect of Spain's economic performance at any time during the twentieth century was the burgeoning of industrial production after 1960. Albert Carreras shows that Spain, whose annual rate of growth of industrial production kept pace with the rest of Europe before the Civil War, lagged badly behind the continental average during the period 1935–50. From 1950 to 1985, however, industrial production south of the Pyrenees averaged 6.85 per cent a year, compared with 4.09 per cent for the rest of Europe. Most dramatically, during the period 1960–74, Spain's industrial output expanded at twice the rate of its European competitors by Carreras's reckoning, averaging 11.13 per cent per annum as against 5.03 per cent (Carreras, 1987).

The slow and irregular growth of Spanish industry in the 1940s and early 1950s can be ascribed to a variety of factors, including the damaging effects on consumer spending of a long sequence of bad harvests, shortages of capital and foreign reserves, difficulties in obtaining imported raw materials and capital goods, energy bottlenecks and the dominant mood of political uncertainty. The year 1953, which coincided with the appearance of sizeable United States aid, constituted a turning point. Over the next quinquennium, industry enjoyed growth rates ranging from seven to 10 per cent annually. Even so, the constraints imposed on the Spanish economy by the Franco regime's autarkic strategy meant that expansion was achieved against a background of galloping inflation and a worsening balance-of-payments position. Once the measures incorporated in the Stabilisation Plan of 1959 had removed most of the obstacles to long-term growth, the country underwent continuous industrial expansion in the period 1961–7, followed by an eight-year phase of stop-go (1967–75), before the oil crisis plunged Spanish manufacturing into a deep recession which lasted for nearly a decade (Carreras, 1987).

What some economic historians see as Spain's long delayed Industrial Revolution had two important effects: it led to a transformation of the country's industrial structure and, in geographical terms, widened her industrial base. An analysis of Spanish input-output tables, which first appeared during the mid-1950s, brings out the relative decline of consumer goods and mining (excluding fuels). In contrast, Spain's industrial take-off in the 1960s centred on three main sectors, which together displayed remarkable vitality. These were: energy products, intermediate goods (not least iron and steel, non-ferrous metals, cement and chemicals), and capital goods – the present-day leading sector of Spanish industry. A sign of changing times was that this expansion of the factory system, along with the establishment of new industries, was marked by an increase in the number and size of manufacturing zones. Most notably, the Madrid conurbation and Valencia became major industrial regions (Fanjul *et al.*, 1975; Martín *et al.*, 1981; Albarracín and Yago, 1986).

The limits of autarky

Once the battles were over, after the spring of 1939, the Francoist authorities focused their attention on the urgent task of national reconstruction. Notwithstanding a shrill peasantist tone among some of the regime's most ardent supporters, it was generally believed in official circles that the economic and political survival of the New State depended on achieving rapid industrialisation. The practical difficulties encountered by Spanish manufacturers in trying to obtain basic raw materials and capital goods, required to get recovery under way, confirmed the new authorities in their commitment to the process of import substitution. As we have seen, this strategy had gained widespread acceptance anyway since the beginning of the century (Velasco, 1982; Braña *et al.*, 1983).

In their illusory quest for autarky, the Spanish authorities adopted a host of policies with regard to industry. These included the regulation of private investment, the foundation of public sector enterprise, quantitative restrictions on foreign trade and the manipulation of the exchange rate (Donges, 1976). To begin with, the Franco regime embarked on a number of indirect measures aimed at encouraging private investment in Spanish industry. Thus, two Acts of 1939 offered a range of incentives and guarantees to new and existing firms. In addition, specific plans were approved for industrial sectors deemed to be of strategic importance, including nitrogen, artificial fibres and vehicles. Companies were legally obliged to obtain prior permission from the Ministry of Industry before constructing, extending or altering the site of any installation. The same ministry was also assigned responsibility for fixing the price of basic manufacturing inputs, such as cement, iron and steel. An aspect of the regime's economic nationalism was that foreign investors were prevented by law from holding more than a quarter stake in Spanish companies, except with special permission from the Council of Ministers.

However, despite their commitment to state interference in the manufacturing process, the Spanish authorities singularly neglected to delineate a coherent set of criteria for making rational decisions. According to Juergen Donges, no industrial priorities were established. Moreover, the Industry Ministry did not undertake a single study on the optimum size or location of firms. In an atmosphere of favouritism and extensive corruption, those entrepreneurs who maintained the most cordial relations with officialdom generally got what they wanted (Donges, 1976).

The failure of Spanish industry to respond to government promptings convinced the policy makers of two factors. Firstly, they were firmly resolved that the market was an ineffective mechanism for the allocation of resources. Secondly, Spain's entrepreneurs were judged to be completely deficient in business acumen. Only through state intervention, it was mistakenly believed, could Spain achieve the desired goals of self-sufficiency and rapid industrialisation. To counter these supposed defects, in September 1941, the *Caudillo* authorised the creation of a public holding company, the *Instituto Nacional de Industria* (INI), which was to be presided over for more than two decades by his boyhood friend, the naval engineer, Juan Antonio Suanzes. The Institute, which was modelled on the *Istituto per la Riconstruzione Industriale*

(IRI), set up by Mussolini in 1933, was charged with promoting and financing industrial development, particularly in those industries concerned with the defence of the realm. Although INI's original brief was to satisfy domestic demand, it was also intended that, in the long run, its component companies would produce a range of exports, thereby earning much-needed foreign currency (Schwartz and González, 1978; Martín Aceña and Comín, 1991).

From its earliest moments, INI's managers showed a marked preference for participating in heavy industry. Under the forthright leadership of Suanzes, efforts were made to consolidate the so-called industrialising trilogy of iron and steel, coal and electricity in a deliberate ploy to eradicate bottlenecks to industrial production. In addition, the Institute's activities were extended to encompass shipbuilding, railway material, oil refining, chemicals, cars, lorries and aircraft. By the end of the 1950s, INI was involved in 56 firms in over 20 branches of industry. Donges records that INI-controlled companies employed two per cent of the Spanish labour force, accounted for approximately seven per cent of the country's gross capital formation and between 30 and 40 per cent of total public investment (Donges, 1976).

Opinions differ greatly with regard to INI's overall contribution to Spain's economic development. Champions of the Institute claim that during the late 1940s and 1950s it built up the basic infrastructure which made possible the rapid industrial growth of the Development era (1960–74) (Braña *et al.*, 1979). By comparison, Schwartz and González, in their history of the INI, stress that a fair number of its projects were undertaken for reasons of national prestige, with little regard to their opportunity cost. For his part, Donges accuses INI of failing to benefit from economies of scale, omitting to provide details of its investment plans, refusing to coordinate its activities with those of the private sector and receiving preferential treatment in the form of tax rebates, lower customs duties, favourable exchange rates and so on (Donges, 1976; Schwartz and González, 1978).

During the 1960s when, in Donges' words, Spain changed its economic strategy from an inward to an outward orientation, INI's privileged status within the manufacturing sector came under challenge. In its report of 1963, *The Economic Development of Spain*, the World Bank recommended that the Institute's future dealings be guided by the principle of subsidiarity. Moreover, the Bank contended, 'INI should not go into any field in which private enterprise has any plans for entering' (International Bank for Reconstruction and Development, 1963; Donges, 1971; Martín Aceña and Comín, 1991).

Evidence of the shortcomings of the Francoist regime's industrial strategy is provided by data on factor size. Donges shows that, on the eve of the Stabilisation Plan, Spain's industrial structure was dominated by a large number of tiny enterprises, which comprised 85 per cent of the total. Even in such sectors as chemicals, basic ferrous metals, machinery and equipment, where the optimum size of firms was generally considered to be over a thousand workers, there was still a predominance of small concerns. Moreover many Spanish firms, most notably in the Catalan textile industry, had not been substantially modernised since their foundation. Chronically low productivity levels, coupled with the inferior quality of their products, meant that few Spanish companies were able to compete on equal terms with their foreign rivals (Donges, 1971).

The industrial boom, 1960–74

Franco's reluctant acceptance of the Stabilisation Plan of 1959 prepared by the technocrats marked a final admission by the old guard that Spain was in no position to bring about rapid industrialisation under conditions of relative isolation. The country's unprecedented rates of industrial expansion in the period 1960–74 were intimately connected to the gradual reinsertion of Spain into the international economic system. Writing in 1971, Juergen Donges attributed the industrial boom of the 1960s to three main developments. Firstly, the trade liberalisation measures initiated by Ullastres in 1959 brought a significant reduction in the effective rate of protection. This factor encouraged the import of capital goods, which in turn contributed to a renovation of much of Spain's outdated capital equipment. Secondly, Donges argues, the technocrats launched a plan of action to promote the export of manufactured goods. Their intentions to do so were signalled by the devaluation of the peseta in 1959. Among the main aspects of the new policy were the provision of export subsidies to producers exempting them from paying indirect taxes on foreign sales, rebates of import duties paid on raw materials, spare parts and capital equipment going into the production of exports, and financial assistance to exporters. Thirdly, Donges highlights the external financing of Spanish industry which, he maintains, reflected a profound change in official attitudes, hitherto hostile, to foreign private capital (Donges, 1971).

Later interpretations of Spain's industrial boom years, while acknowledging the liberalising achievements of Ullastres and his successors, argue that Spain's industrialisation policy in the 1960s was still resolutely protectionist. The Spanish government's failure to further reduce the country's relatively high tariff barriers, they contend, encouraged manufacturers to settle for easy picking in the domestic market. Economists such as José Antonio Martínez Serrano and Rafael Myro cite a combination of factors as contributing to the 1960s boom, including the availability of cheap and abundant supplies of energy, the constant stream of rural and female labour which made its way into the factories and workshops, and the provision of external finance in the shape of foreign investment, emigrant remittances and earnings from foreign tourism. Foreign investment was of crucial importance to the industrialisation process, not least because of Spanish industry's unwillingness to undertake research and development (Martínez Serrano *et al.*, 1982; Braña *et al.*, 1984; Myro, 1988).

In an attempt to tackle the longstanding weaknesses of the reduced dimension of enterprises, shortage of capital, technological backwardness and low productivity, Spain's policy makers pursued a strategy of industrial concentration. A variety of inducements and exemptions were dangled in front of companies to encourage mergers and takeovers. These initiatives met with a limited amount of success. The concentration of production into bigger units, with resulting economies of scale, was especially important in metallurgy, chemicals, construction and foodstuffs. Even so, Fernando Maravall found that between 1964 and 1968, growth rates were marginally higher in medium-sized enterprises than in large firms. For the period 1968–73, he discovered that the largest firms were also those which achieved the highest rates of growth, probably due to their capacity to obtain finance on the most favourable terms. Maravall also concludes that there was little correlation between the size of industrial companies and their ability to secure economies of scale, above all because many large firms favoured a multi-plant structure (Maravall, 1976).

Crisis and restructuring

In Spain, as in most other industrial nations, the energy crisis of the second half of the 1970s triggered off a pronounced deceleration in industrial growth. However, in the Spanish case, the collapse was even more emphatic than among its competitors. During the period 1975–80, Spain, whose fastest-growing industries (chemicals, iron and steel, cement) were extremely energy intensive, tumbled from next to the top of the international league table of industrial growth to not far from bottom place.

A study into the performance of Spanish industry in the period 1970–84 by Jesús Albarracín and Alfonso Yago demonstrates that industrial output south of the Pyrenees rose by 45 per cent overall between 1970 and 1974, an annual increase of 9.7 per cent. This figure represented twice the industrial growth rate attained in the United States, Japan and Italy and four times that of the United Kingdom and West Germany. In marked contrast, from 1974 to 1979, Spain's industrial output rose by a miserable 5.7 per cent in total, compared with around 10 per cent in France, West Germany, Italy and the United Kingdom and 18 per cent in the United States and Japan (Albarracín and Yago, 1986). After a short-lived recovery in 1980, Spanish industry grew only slowly in the first half of the 1980s, before fortunes recovered in the period 1986–9 when the increase in industrial output fluctuated between 3.1 and 4.6 per cent per annum. In 1990, it fell to zero (Banco Bilbao Vizcaya, 1992).

The ten-year industrial depression, which essentially reflected a drop in domestic demand, gave rise to a spate of company bankruptcies and factory closures. Many employers attempted to respond to the crisis by cutting their payrolls. Yet, in the political turmoil and uncertainty of the late 1970s, this course of action often proved difficult. On the one hand, Spain's newly-legalised trade unions adopted a militant stance designed to safeguard employment among their membership. On the other hand, employers' organisations complained that they were prevented from taking effective countermeasures as a result of paternalist legislation inherited from the former dictatorship. Even so, a million jobs were lost in industry between 1975 and 1985, while the labour force contracted from 3.6 millions to 2.6 millions (Salmon, 1991).

Both Donges and Myro emphasise that one of the most significant and potentially far-reaching developments in the industrial sector in the late 1970s and early 1980s was the search for external outlets by Spanish manufacturers, in compensation for the depressed state of the home market. Their task was not made any easier due to fierce competition from two directions: advanced nations in a similar situation to Spain and the Newly-Industrialising Countries, which had the advantage of lower wage costs. The main thrust of the NICs' export offensive came in labour-intensive products, including textiles and footwear. In addition, Spanish industry had to face a daunting challenge in a range of items, notably electrical appliances, cars, plastics and ships. Nonetheless, against fairly formidable odds, the period 1975–85 witnessed a remarkable achievement by the nation's manufacturers who built up new markets for their products. Above all, Spain performed well in sectors of intermediate technology; for example, vehicles, machine tools and avionics. Yet, when internal demand began to show greater buoyancy in the second half of the 1980s, Spanish industrialists again stood accused of relying on the restricted home market and letting slip markets recently captured abroad (Donges, 1983; Myro, 1988).

After a disturbing lapse of time, the authorities in Madrid at last began to react to the recession in the industrial sector. Their main form of response to Spain's chronic deindustrialisation was an attempt to restructure manufacturing through a policy known as industrial reconversion. As Keith Salmon comments, official reaction to the industrial slump was much tardier than in most other countries. Indeed, in sectors such as steel and shipbuilding, large investment programmes continued to be encouraged right up to the end of the 1970s, even though demand had plummeted worldwide (Salmon, 1991). Vital decisions on cutbacks or restructuring were frequently postponed because the Spanish authorities thought it politically expedient to mollify powerful vested interests, most notably the banks, trade unions and regionalist parties. Before the Socialists took office in October 1982 and for a time afterwards, INI was utilised by successive administrations as a gigantic dustbin for company crashes in the private sector, at great expense to the taxpayer (Martín Aceña and Comín, 1991).

The objectives of Spain's industrial reconversion policy varied according to the difficulties which afflicted a particular firm or industry. They included the elimination of excess capacity, an attempt to incorporate improvements in technology, design and quality, and efforts to reduce production costs in order to make Spanish goods more competitive in international markets (Albentosa, 1985; Navarro Arancegui, 1989).

The process got under way in 1979 when the Suárez government began talking to individual companies with a view to restructuring their production. Starting in 1980, a series of so-called reconversion decrees were approved aimed at solving the underlying problems of specific sectors. Among other measures, tax incentives were offered to firms which considered amalgamation. Industries affected by the legislation included iron and steel, shipbuilding, textiles, footwear and electronic components. Yet, according to Salmon, a good deal of the state transfers for industrial reconversion before 1982 went to absorb losses rather than to tackle underlying disequilibria. The same author also tells us that the frantic activity of the González Socialist administration, culminating in the Law of Reconversion and Reindustrialisation of 1984, owed a great deal to the imminence of Spain's entry into the European Community. Ministers, he argues, recognised that EC membership would entail not only increased competition but also the adoption of Community regulations which limited state assistance to industry. During the period 1984–6, the cost of Spain's reconversion plan was put at 1,000 billion pesetas, a large part of which was directed towards the iron and steel industry. Yet industrial reconversion was far from painless. The 1984 plan brought the loss of 85,000 jobs over the next five years, nine-tenths of them in iron and steel, shipbuilding, textiles and domestic appliances (Albentosa, 1985; Navarro Arancegui, 1989; Salmon, 1991).

6
Energy

During the half century since the end of the conflict of 1936–9, the question of energy requirements troubled the Spanish authorities on two separate occasions. Firstly, during the 1940s and the first half of the following decade, consumers – both domestic and industrial – suffered the combined effects of acute problems in securing adequate supplies of imported oil along with cuts in the electricity supply. On the second occasion, which resulted from OPEC's decision in 1973 to employ the oil weapon, the ailing dictatorship and its democratic successors were confronted almost overnight with the nation's perilous dependence on imported energy. Above all, as we have seen, Spain's rapid industrialisation in the period 1960–74 was heavily concentrated on the impressive expansion of the energy-intensive heavy goods sector. Carles Sudrià, in a pioneering survey article on energy in Spain, distinguishes three distinct phases since the Civil War: war, autarky and energy shortages (1936–55), the age of oil (1955–73) and the subsequent energy crisis and its aftermath (Sudrià, 1987). Sudrià's periodisation will provide the framework for the rest of this chapter.

Bottlenecks to energy supply, 1939–55

By comparison with its advanced neighbours to the north, Spain, with its arrested industrial development and low level of urbanisation, consumed relatively limited amounts of energy per capita in the immediate post-civil-war years.

At the beginning of the Franco era, almost nine-tenths of

Spain's energy consumption was coal-based. After a severe inter-ruption to mining activities in Asturias, which traditionally ac-counted for approximately three-fifths of the domestic output, production returned to normality in 1939. Yet, in terms of overall energy needs, Spain did possess an Achilles heel, in the shape of oil and oil derivatives. During the three-year conflict, the Nationalist zone was remarkably successful in obtaining vital supplies of oil for its armies from the Texas Oil Company (Texaco) which became the leading provider of the insurgent forces. Even so, the pro-Axis stance of the Franco regime throughout World War II persuaded the Allies, especially the United States, to treat oil supply as a bargaining counter in their commercial relations with Spain. As a consequence of the wartime embargo, Spain, which consumed one million tonnes of oil products in 1940, was allotted only 350,000 tonnes in 1942. Not until 1946 was the 1940 level of consumption re-established. After the Armistice, the United Nations' diplomatic boycott of the Franco regime in March 1946, combined with shortages of foreign currency with which to purchase supplies, exacerbated an already difficult situation. It was the amelioration of Spain's balance-of-payments position in the mid-1950s, coin-ciding with the arrival of American aid, which at last permitted the country to satisfy its growing appetite for imported oil. Despite costly attempts by the *Instituto Nacional de Industria* to manufacture an *ersatz* petroleum – known as *gasógeno* – from indigenous coal deposits, the shortage of oil had particularly deleterious effects on transportation. Rising transport costs in turn contributed to an increase in the price of foodstuffs and consumer goods and were a key element in Spain's runaway inflation of the late 1940s (García Alonso, 1983; Sudrià, 1987).

After 1944, electrical power cuts became a regular occurrence, as the countryside and cities were plunged into total or partial darkness and manufacturing production was forced to grind to a halt. The problem persisted well into the next decade. Sudrià calculates that in the period 1944–54, demand for electricity south of the Pyrenees exceeded supply by roughly ten per cent. Succes-sive troughs were experienced in 1945 and 1949 when shortfalls in the provision of electricity stood at 33 per cent and 27 per cent respectively. The important contribution of hydro-electric power within overall electricity supply meant that Spanish consumers were the perennial victims of the 'enduring drought' during the 1940s, since the power stations in the Pyrenees were subject to sporadic and inadequate rainfall. For his part, Sudrià places the blame for the shortfall in electricity supply fairly and squarely on the ill-considered interventionist policies of the dictatorship which prevented the power companies from raising their charges to customers before 1951, thereby discouraging further investment. The main repercussions of the power cuts were felt in the leading industrial regions of Catalonia and the Basque Country where factories were often obliged to shut down their production for weeks and even months on end (Ribas i Massana, 1978; Sudrià, 1987, 1988a).

An age of cheap oil imports

Bottlenecks to energy supply south of the Pyrenees were by and large eradicated in the late 1950s. Between 1955 and 1973, Spain's annual consumption of energy went up by 6.9 per cent. Most dramatically, the period 1965–73 saw energy consumption escalate by 8.9 per cent a year, over two points above the rate of growth of GDP. The prime cause of this increase was the seemingly insatiable demands of manufacturing industry. Thus, on the eve of the Yom Kippur War in 1973, 52.5 per cent of the country's energy consumption was accounted for by the secondary sector. Moreover, the most rapid increase in demand came from industries which used up more than their proportionate share of energy; notably, chemicals, metallurgy, shipbuilding and cement. In addition, industry's incorporation of labour-saving technology into the manufacturing process brought about a significant expansion in the consumption of energy per unit of production. After industry, transport – especially road transport – was responsible for the second largest increase in consumption, thanks largely to the spread of the petrol-guzzling heavy lorry at the expense of Spain's slow and inefficient railway network. Notwithstanding the remarkable shift of population from rural Spain to the big conurbations at this time, and the rise in living standards, domestic consumption of energy accounted for only one-tenth of the total in 1973.

With regard to the relative share of energy consumption, the most significant change which occurred during the Development Years was Spain's dramatic switch from home-produced coal to imported oil. According to José María García Alonso, oil, which was both cheaper and more abundant, provided 67.2 per cent of national energy requirements in 1973, as against a mere 27.9 per cent in 1960. Altogether, during this fourteen-year period, oil consumption expanded more than sixfold. Over the same time-span, the contribution of coal to total energy requirements slumped from 47.0 per cent to 17.3 per cent (García Alonso, 1983).

Little effort was made to prospect for oil either inside the peninsula or offshore. Meanwhile Spain, which from the late 1940s built a number of coastal refineries at Corunna, Castellón, Huelva, Bilbao, Algeciras, Puertollano and Escombreras, became a net exporter of oil-based products (Marín Quemada, 1978; Sudrià, 1988b).

Next to oil, energy consumption increased most rapidly in the electricity sector, which boasted an annual average growth rate of 11 per cent during the period of 1960–73. Before the mid-1960s, priority in electricity supply was given to hydro-electric power. Official interest also centred on the erection of coal-fired power stations. Yet, since the cost of extracting Spanish coal rose sharply because of geological problems while fuel oil was relatively cheaper, a second generation of power stations, fired by oil, came into being. Elsewhere, as Juan Iranzo testifies, the country's unquenchable demand for energy stimulated mounting investment in nuclear power. The first nuclear-power station to enter into production was the José Cabrera Zorita in Guadalajara in 1969. It was joined in 1971 by the Santa María de Garoña (Burgos) followed by the Vandellós I (Tarragona) in 1972. This first wave of nuclear-power stations possessed a combined generating capacity of 1,200 megawatts (Iranzo, 1984; Sudrià, 1987; Salmon, 1991).

To complete the picture of Spain's energy supplies, after 1969 natural gas was brought to the peninsula from Algeria. Lack of interest by the central authorities coincided with a poor rate of expansion, except in Catalonia. The first regasification plant was constructed in Barcelona in 1971, where the pipelines conveying town gas was converted to natural gas. Yet, throughout the next decade, the contribution of natural gas to Spain's total energy requirements stayed well below the EC average (Sudrià, 1988a; Rivero, 1989; Salmon, 1991).

Overall, as a result of the changes mentioned above, the proportion of Spain's total demand for primary energy supplies satisfied by domestic products fell from 62 per cent in 1963 to 28 per cent in 1973. Moreover, oil now supplied two-thirds of the country's energy needs. Since as much as 98 per cent of the oil consumed in Spain was imported, the implications of the country's massive external dependence on a single commodity soon became all too apparent (Iranzo, 1984).

The oil crisis and energy planning

The sharp and unexpected rise in the price of crude oil in the autumn of 1973, after two decades of cheap energy, heralded the emergence of a series of problems which threatened the economic stability of western economies during the late 1970s and beyond. Prominent among these problems were a decline in growth rates, rampant inflation and widening trade gaps. Spain, with its immense reliance on oil imports, was not immune from the general trend. However, while the majority of nations acted quickly to introduce a series of countermeasures aimed at stemming the consumption of oil and securing significant energy savings in general, the Madrid government was slow to implement similar policies. Worse still, in a forlorn attempt to insulate the Iberian nation from the international situation and to avert social problems at home, the Spanish authorities deluded themselves into believing that the problems of the oil market were nothing more than a passing phenomenon. Thus, ministers ruled out structural readjustments. To the bewilderment of informed opinion, successive increases in the price of oil agreed by the OPEC producers, were in part absorbed by the Spanish Exchequer which reduced the amount of tax paid on oil products. As a result, while the cost of crude oil acquired by Spanish refineries soared more than fivefold between 1973 and 1978, the domestic price of fuel oil – the leading subproduct of oil – went up by no more than a factor of 2.6. This fundamental error of the authorities is demonstrated by the fact that, far from achieving energy savings or the substitution of imported oil by domestically-obtained products, the reverse situation occurred. During the period 1973–8, oil consumption in Spain drifted upwards by nearly a third (Sudrià, 1988b).

How did the Spanish authorities formulate energy policy in the long-run? Before the appearance of the oil crisis in 1973, energy forecasting south of the Pyrenees was largely confined to sectoral planning and the gathering of statistical data for incorporation into the Development Plans. Throughout 1974, however, Francoist policy makers worked on the preparation of a long-term energy plan whose main objectives were the diversification of energy supply and a reduction in the overall contribution of oil in order to tackle the troublesome issue of Spain's external dependence. Spain's first national energy plan, to be called PEN–75 (*Plan Energético Nacional*), argued that a strong impulse be given to nuclear power and also to the spread of natural gas. However, given the prevailing atmosphere of political instability which followed the death of the dictator, none of the planners' recommendations were acted upon. A lengthy delay ensued until the first *Cortes* of the new democracy approved a second energy plan in 1979, dubbed PEN–78. Although the latter sensibly scaled down previous forecasts of Spain's demand for energy, it nevertheless predicted an appreciable increase in the consumption of energy over the period 1978–87, accompanied by a gradual diminution in the nation's dependence on imported oil. With a growing awareness of world events, the planners argued that in future, all increases in the price of crude oil should be passed on to the consumer. Even so, PEN–78 was almost immediately blown off course by the second oil crisis of 1979 which led to a trebling of the price of crude oil within a few months. A revision of the second energy plan in 1981 predicted a further decline in the demand for energy and called for an enhanced substitution of coal and nuclear power for oil. Finally, when the Socialists won power in 1982, they undertook an even more detailed review of the energy situation in Spain, later to appear as PEN–84. The country's third energy plan forecast still greater reductions in the long-term demand for energy. It therefore brought a halt to the construction of some of Spain's nuclear plants. PEN–84 also gained widespread approval among specialists for its proposals to rationalise the various energy subsectors, especially electricity supply (Iranzo, 1984; Sudrià, 1988b; Rivero, 1989).

Early signs suggest that the planners are finally having an impact. In his study of energy policy during the period 1980–7, Pedro Rivero maintains that Spain's vulnerability with regard to the provision of energy has diminished and that greater efficiency in the areas of generation and consumption, along with a more rational use of available resources, has been achieved (Rivero, 1989).

7
The service sector

The service sector, also known as the 'tertiary' or 'residual' sector, has long been a Cinderella subject within the sphere of economic investigation. In Spain, as elsewhere, despite the growing importance of services in recent decades, there have been few detailed and comprehensive studies. Scholarly research in contemporary Spanish economic history has tended to focus on the shift from agriculture to industry.

In global terms, the process of rapid tertiary expansion got under way in the United States after 1945. Subsequently, other industrialised nations followed the American pattern, often with a significant time lag. In 1968, the economist Victor Fuchs coined the phrase 'service economy' to describe a situation where more than half of a country's labour force was employed in activities other than farming, forestry, fisheries, mining and manufacturing (Fuchs, 1968).

Using Fuchs's criteria, Spain can be said to have joined the ranks of the world's service economies in 1981. At the beginning of the present decade, the OECD average for employment in the service sector was 62 per cent. In certain countries, including Great Britain, Belgium, the United States, Canada and Australia, the proportion was as high as 70 per cent. By comparison, Spain trailed several percentage points behind. According to Juan Ramón Cuadrado, in 1990, 54.2 per cent of the Spanish working population was engaged in the various pursuits which together comprise the tertiary sector, among them commerce, transport, tourism, financial services, education, health and social services. In terms of the sector's contribution to Spain's GDP, services accounted for about three-fifths in 1990: i.e., 61.1 per cent, measured at current prices, or 58.3 per cent when calculated at constant 1980 prices (Cuadrado, 1988, 1990; Sáez, 1990).

South of the Pyrenees, the emergence of a dominant service sector, sometimes referred to by economists as *tertialisation*, coincided with the stage of rapid industrialisation after the 1959 Stabilisation Plan. Cuadrado attributes the rapid tertiary growth to three basic factors: the spread of mass tourism along the *costas*, large scale urbanisation and rising living standards (Cuadrado, 1988, 1990).

Unlike agriculture, which experienced a marked contraction in terms of employment and its contribution to GDP from the late 1950s onwards, or the manufacturing sector, where the process of deindustrialisation got under way after 1975, services never ceased to gain weight within the Spanish economy. In addition, the tertiary sector as a whole proved less vulnerable to cyclical fluctuations than its two counterparts. In this respect, services constituted an important stabilising element, particularly during the troubled times of the late 1970s and early 1980s. This does not mean that the progress of the tertiary sector was a smooth one in all its component parts. Not all of its branches were exempt from recession and rising unemployment (Cuadrado, 1990).

Cuadrado distinguishes three main stages in the progress of Spain's service sector since 1960 – the two previous decades remain largely uncharted territory. Firstly, during the boom years of 1960–74, most branches of the tertiary sector experienced fast and extensive growth, with a small number of exceptions such as personal and domestic services. Secondly, the depression decade of 1975–85 witnessed modest yet welcome expansion. Finally, the resurgence of the Spanish economy after the mid-1980s led to a spectacular upsurge in employment opportunities in services (Cuadrado, 1988).

In the aftermath of the Stabilisation Plan, Spain's tertiary sector took off in the shadow of the remarkable burgeoning of manufacturing industry and construction. Between 1960 and 1973, annual growth rates in services averaged a respectable 6.8 per cent, while the sector's contribution to GDP rose from 40.8 per cent to 49.5 per cent. Another noted feature of the tertiary sector was its extraordinary capacity to generate additional employment. In the period 1960–73, a further 1.78 million jobs were created, while the proportion of Spain's labour force occupied in services went up from 28.3 per cent to 38.5 per cent. Even so, at the conclusion of this phase of expansion, Spain remained well behind the average for OECD countries where the tertiary sector accounted for over half of the registered labour force.

This gap was significantly narrowed in the decade after 1975. Ten years later, 50.8 per cent of Spain's working population was employed in services, compared with an average of 57.2 per cent for the European Community and 57.3 per cent in the OECD. In fact, the tertiary sector in Spain weathered the economic recession far more effectively than agriculture or industry. Felipe Sáez calculates that, for the sector as a whole, there was a net gain of 165,000 jobs during the period 1975–85. Over the same timespan, significant structural changes took place within the sector. As a result of the economic recession, thousands of jobs were lost in employment shake outs in private-sector service activities, most notably in shipping, hotels, catering, transport and communications. In contrast, thanks to the spread of political and administrative institutions at national, regional and local levels, there were compensating gains in employment in public administration, social services and education (Sáez, 1990).

More unambiguously, the second half of the 1980s saw a renewed upsurge in the fortunes of the service sector. Between 1985 and 1990, 1.5 million additional jobs were created, with tourism, the hotel trade and commerce in the vanguard. Even so, not all commentators view this expansion as an unqualified success story. Cuadrado, for example, stresses that one half of these 'new' jobs were either part-time or temporary in nature. This was especially true in such areas as the tourist trade, hotels and catering where seasonal employment predominated, especially in coastal regions. Moreover, few of the additional jobs required professional qualifications. Many employees in the service sector, not least women workers, had to live on wages well below the national average. In contrast, the expansion of the financial sector involved the appointment of skilled personnel and offered the prospect of further professional training. However, in line with similar developments elsewhere, a heated discussion took place in Spain as to whether the expansion of employment in the service sector entailed the provision of *real* jobs or was little more than a statistical fiction favoured by governments in order to camouflage the unemployment statistics (Cuadrado, 1990; Banco Bilbao Vizcaya, 1992).

One unsatisfactory feature of the consolidation of the tertiary sector in Spain was its uneven impact in geographical terms. For example, in 1985, only six of the country's seventeen autonomous communities had more than half of their working population engaged in services. These six were, in order of importance, Madrid, the Balearic Islands, the Canary Islands, Andalusia, Murcia and Valencia. At the opposite end of the scale, in Galicia, Asturias and Castilla-La Mancha only 35.5 per cent, 42.0 per cent and 42.5 per cent respectively of the working population were employed in services. As Cuadrado argues, apart from Madrid with its strong links with the administration, the essential reason for this disparity lay in the relative importance of tourism, leisure activities and associated developments in financial services, transport and commerce within the sector. Cuadrado also bemoans the fact that in the recession-hit industrial regions of the north (Asturias, Cantabria and the Basque Country) which had little tourism infrastructure, the tertiary sector was in no position to perform a major compensatory role during the crisis of 1975–85, as it did in Catalonia (particularly Barcelona) and Madrid (Cuadrado, 1990).

A more positive aspect of the service sector, the contribution of receipts from foreign tourism to Spain's balance of payments, is dealt with in the next chapter.

8
Foreign trade

The Stabilisation Plan of 1959, which set out the Franco regime's commitment to liberalise the country's economic relations with the rest of the world, constitutes a vital turning point in the economic history of twentieth-century Spain. After the failures and disappointments of the previous two decades of autarkic development, based on a series of costly attempts at import substitution, the new breed of technocratic ministers, appointed in 1957, embarked on a course of action designed to incorporate the Spanish economy into the resurgent international system. Throughout the period 1939–59, a combination of the regime's ideological adherence to economic nationalism, bureaucratic inertia and the entrenched protectionist sentiments of powerful farming and industrial lobbies, frustrated any attempt, whether internal or external in origin, to open up Spain to the benefits of foreign trade and inward investment. The latter option, Ramón Tamames contends, was available to Spanish policy makers at least five years before the elaboration of the Stabilisation Plan. Had Trade Minister Manuel Arburúa shown more than a rhetorical commitment in the mid-1950s to opening up the Spanish economy, he might reasonably have expected enthusiastic support from the US administration, at that time providing the Franco regime with all-important foreign aid (Tamames, 1970; Gámir, 1980).

Arburúa's miserable failure to stimulate sufficient exports, particularly manufactures, to finance imports of raw materials and capital goods, together with the exhaustion of American aid after 1956, revealed the bankruptcy of Francoist economic policy. However, as Manuel-Jesús González argues, only the sudden awareness in the summer of 1959 of the likelihood of Spain's economic and political collapse, together with the persuasive skills of Finance Minister Mariano Navarro Rubio, finally convinced the obstinate *Caudillo* that his regime's goal of self-sufficiency was completely unattainable (González, 1979).

Trade liberalisation

José Antonio Alonso distinguishes three main phases of trade liberalisation in the wake of the Stabilisation Plan: 1959–66, 1970–75 and 1977–80. To these must be added changes associated with Spain's membership of the European Community since 1986. Yet, as Alonso shows, the process of liberalising Spain's foreign trading relations was far from plain sailing. The intervening years were interrupted by a series of setbacks and delays due to such factors as pressures from a variety of vested interests, the negative repercussions of stop-go policies and balance-of-payments difficulties. In particular, early on, the recession of 1966–7 brought a near paralysis to further negotiations. Fortunately, Spain's liberal reformers benefited from invaluable help and encouragement from the leading international bodies, not least the International Monetary Fund, the World Bank, the OECD, the European Common Market, GATT and EFTA (Alonso, 1988).

The starting point for Spain's first emphatic phase of trade liberalisation this century was the new tariff approved in May 1960. This measure, which followed three years of hard bargaining, reasserted the normal pre-eminent place of the tariff within commercial policy. After the depression of the 1930s, this role was usurped by a mixed bag of interventionist devices, including quotas, import licences, exchange controls and differential exchange rates. For its part, the Spanish administration pledged itself to remove all duties on approximately half of the goods imported from OECD countries. Other imports were to be subject to a less stringent regime of customs duties. Above all, what differentiated Commerce Minister Ullastres from earlier holders of that portfolio under Franco was the former's genuine rejection of the strategy of import substitution and his unequivocal commitment to extending Spain's foreign trade relations. Even so, commentators like Alonso emphasise the high degree of initial protection levied on items excluded from arrangements with the OECD. In addition, the Minister's successors are charged with responsibility for bringing about an unnecessarily complicated set of trading agreements, mainly due to the plethora of exemptions and rebates resulting from their cherished discretionary powers. By the mid-1970s, Alonso tells us, the value of these concessions more than exceeded the total sum of revenue collected by the Spanish customs (Alonso, 1988).

The second phase of trade liberalisation followed the signing of the Luxembourg Accord of July 1970 with the European Common Market, the terms of which were in general more favourable to Spain. Although the long-term goal of this agreement was the establishment of unrestrained free trade in agricultural and industrial products between Spain and the 'Six', in the short-run, the former profited from a generous reduction in the Common Market's external tariff. In return, Spain offered only moderate concessions on imports from the 'Six'. Later in 1972–3, further liberalising measures were adopted, largely with the intention of containing domestic inflation.

Finally, the third phase of trade liberalisation, between 1977 and 1980, coincided with a run of favourable trade figures. An agreement with the European Free Trade Area provided that Spain extend to EFTA similar terms to those concluded in the 1970 Accord with the Common Market. Simultaneously, under the aegis of the Tokyo Round of the General Agreement on Tariffs and Trade, Spain committed itself to a 40 per cent lowering of import duties along with staged reductions between 1979 and 1987 (Alonso, 1988; Arroyo Ilera, 1988).

Although Spain's foreign trade policy at this time is nowadays viewed as erring on the side of caution, the measures described above resulted in a significant dismantling of the barriers to international trade. In all three phases, the level of nominal protection dropped perceptibly: from 16.5 to 11.2 per cent between 1960 and 1966, 9.5 to 6.8 per cent (1970–4) and 8.2 to 6.1 per cent (1977–80). Between 1980 and the country's accession to the European Community in 1986 – which implied the removal of duties by both parties by the end of 1992 – the level of protection stabilised at roughly five per cent. Even so, before 1986 nominal protection remained high in a number of industries, not least shoes, furniture and car production (Alonso, 1988).

Trade expansion and its geographical distribution

Following the ending of the Franco regime's obsession with autarky, the authorities began to consider the expansion of international trade as a *sine qua non* for the achievement of uninterrupted industrial development south of the Pyrenees. Between 1964 and 1986, Spain's foreign trade expanded by approximately ten per cent a year in real terms, compared with an average annual increase of 7.8 per cent for the OECD. Exports, which moved ahead after the devaluation of the peseta in 1967, in the wake of Britain's devaluation of sterling, stayed buoyant throughout the next two decades. In contrast, imports made halting progress. They grew most rapidly before 1973, when imported capital goods played a crucial role in the re-equipment of Spanish industry. From 1973 to 1985, the reversal of Spain's economic fortunes brought a reduced rate of growth of imports. After 1985, a variety of factors, including rising domestic demand, a strong peseta and the further liberalisation of foreign trade consequent upon Spain's EC membership, led to another upturn in imports (Alonso, 1988).

The composition of Spain's foreign trade over the past three decades clearly reflects the country's changing economic structure. At the beginning of the 1960s, for example, over half of Spanish exports consisted of agricultural produce, above all fruit, wines, oil and vegetables. By the early 1980s, manufactures accounted for over seven-tenths of exports by value. Moreover, the consolidation of the manufacturing sector was indicated by a marked concentration on specific types of imports. Martínez Serrano and his team, comparing Spanish trade in 1964 and 1980, show that four-fifths of Spain's imports in these two years consisted of raw materials, energy products, intermediate and capital goods (Martínez Serrano *et al.*, 1982).

In terms of the geographical distribution of Spain's foreign trade, the most remarkable feature during the period after the Luxembourg Accord of 1970 was the strengthening of trade with the European Community. This was particularly true of exports.

In 1973, for example, 43.2 per cent of Spain's imports and 48.5 per cent of exports were with the 'Nine'. Twelve years later in 1985, on the eve of Spanish accession to the European Community, imports from the EC accounted for 36.8 per cent of the total, while exports stood at 52.2 per cent. Subsequently, EC membership had pronounced effects on the composition of Spain's main trading partners. Thus, in 1990, the Community was responsible for 59.2 per cent of Spain's imports and 68.9 per cent of her exports (Alonso, 1988; Banco Bilbao Vizcaya, 1991).

Tourism, emigrant remittances and foreign investment

Apart from achieving tiny surpluses in her balance of merchandise trade in 1951 and 1952, due largely to abundant harvests, and again in 1960, because of the depressive effects on imports of the 1959 Stabilisation Plan, Spain ran up an almost unbroken series of trade deficits after the Civil War. Until the mid 1980s, shortfalls in Spain's merchandise trade were offset by surpluses in the invisible account in services and transfers. Most importantly, the country built up substantial positive balances on the tourism account while at the same time benefiting from a net inflow of foreign investment. However, as Keith Salmon points out, after 1987, Spain's current account moved sharply into the red. This worrying predicament, Salmon argues, was largely the result of a widening trade gap coupled with a deterioration in the invisible account as tourism revenues stagnated and expenditure by Spanish holidaymakers abroad took off (Salmon, 1991).

Throughout the 1960s and early 1970s, the contribution of foreign tourism to the country's balance of payments was of vital importance. Between 1959 and 1973, the number of foreign visitors, attracted in the main by Spain's warm climate and cheap alcohol, rose more than eightfold, from 4.2 millions to 34.6 millions. More significantly, receipts soared from $129 million to $3,091 million over the same period. According to an OECD report, as early as 1961, Spain's dependence on earnings from foreign tourism in her balance of payments was greater than any other nation. Between 1961 and 1969, receipts from tourism covered about three-quarters of the trade deficit. By the early

1970s, they more or less wiped out the country's huge visible deficit. This fortuitous situation was dramatically reversed in 1973 when the cost of Spain's imports of crude oil rocketed. Even so, during two subsequent brief periods (1978–9 and 1984–7), income from foreign holidaymakers compensated for the whole of Spain's visible deficit (Harrison, 1985; Alonso, 1988; Banco Bilbao Vizcaya, 1990).

Receipts from Spanish migrants working abroad, although important, played a secondary role in Spain's balance of payments. Josep Fontana and Jordi Nadal calculate that between 1962 and 1971, emigrant remittances offset 17.9 per cent of the total visible deficit, roughly one-third of the contribution of tourism. After the mid 1970s, when the European recession provoked the return of tens of thousands of Spanish migrant workers to the peninsula, emigrant remittances were less significant (Fontana and Nadal, 1976).

Foreign investment in the Spanish economy was facilitated by legislation of 1959 which offered generous incentives and guarantees to outside investors. New regulations allowed foreign nationals to invest in a Spanish company up to half of its total capital without first having to obtain official approval. The Spanish authorities also sanctioned the repatriation of dividends, capital and asset appreciation from such investments. Where foreign investors wished to subscribe in the shares of a company, over fifty per cent of whose social capital was held by non-residents, prior approval of the Council of Ministers was required (Donges, 1976).

Even so, according to Salmon, foreign investment was very small by OECD standards during the 1960s. During the period 1970–85, it rose at a modest pace. In 1986, however, the combined effects of EC membership, low labour costs, financial and tax incentives, political stability and an overvalued peseta caused net inward investment to soar by 75 per cent. It continued to grow rapidly throughout the rest of the decade. By 1989, net inward investment, which stood at $16.6 billion, was roughly equivalent to three per cent of Spain's GDP (Salmon, 1991).

With regard to its composition, before 1986, the largest component of gross inward investment was accounted for by direct investment – defined as acquisitions of twenty per cent or more in a Spanish company. Fernando Jiménez Latorre and Luis de

Guindós calculate that between 1973 and 1984, 43.6 per cent of all foreign investment fell into this category. However, during the second half of the 1980s, portfolio investment, such as the purchase of treasury bills, dominated new investment, while investments in property grew at a steady pace throughout the decade (Jiménez Latorre and Guindós, 1985; Rodríguez de Pablo, 1988).

9
The financial system

Financial reconstitution, cheap money and the status quo

One of the most pressing tasks confronting the victorious Franco regime in April 1939 was the reconstitution of Spain's financial system, split into two by the Civil War. During the conflict, the monetary authorities in both zones resorted to a variety of devices to pay for their costly campaigns. From the beginning, the Republican government attempted to bring in as much revenue as possible for its war effort by the sale of treasury bills. However, after two years of unbridled inflation, its citizens were unwilling to subscribe to official issues bearing low rates of interest. Hence, the Republican Exchequer came to depend to a large extent on loans from the Bank of Spain. In his authoritative contribution to the Bank of Spain's official history, published in 1970, Juan Sardà shows, by reference to the institution's balance sheets, that during the Civil War the so-called red Treasury borrowed as much as 22,740 million pesetas from its central bank. More revealingly, the same author describes how in November 1936, when the rebel forces were on the outskirts of Madrid, Finance Minister Juan Negrín authorised the transfer of Spain's gold reserves, valued at approximately $500 million, from the vaults of the Bank of Spain to the Soviet Union for safekeeping. Sardà's unequivocal statement that the world's fourth largest gold reserve was spent in its entirety on the purchase of armaments and other materials for the defeated Republic, caused such a stir that the Franco regime went so far as to remove from circulation a widely-acclaimed volume which appeared under the imprimatur of its own central bank. Meanwhile, for their part, the insurgents also tried to finance their military rebellion from internal sources. Throughout the conflict, the Nationalist Bank of Spain, established in Burgos in September 1936, made loans of 10,100 million pesetas to the rebel Exchequer. Even so, it is commonly accepted that the triumph of the Spanish Right owed a great deal to foreign support. The American historian Robert Whealey calculates that the Axis powers furnished Franco with $569 million, while the democracies provided the insurgents with aid totalling $76 million (Sardà, 1970; Whealey, 1977).

As Sardà recounts, it took the New Order's first Finance Minister, José Larraz, almost three years to liquidate the worrying financial situation which he inherited after the ending of the hostilities. Among the problems he had to tackle were the unification of the two central banks, the consolidation of the enlarged public debt of both camps, determining the level of the money supply and setting in motion a new post-civil war monetary and financial order (Sardà, 1970).

Most commentators, although critical of subsequent developments, applaud Larraz's painstaking efforts at this stage. Above all, the Minister gets credit for carrying out a complex technical operation without provoking rampant inflation. To this effect, an Act of December 1939 (the *Ley de Desbloqueo*) substantially reduced the liabilities of the central bank which derived from its operations in the Republican zone after 18 July 1936. At the same time, the Francoist authorities refused to accept as legal tender those banknotes issued by the 'Marxist' government after the outbreak of civil war. Such measures lead Ramón Tamames to charge the New Order with introducing a law for the victors (Tamames, 1973; Martín Aceña, 1991).

A minor achievement of Larraz was the recovery from neighbouring France of the remainder of Spain's gold reserves. This consignment, valued at 497 million pesetas, was deposited at the Bank of France's branch at Mont de Marsan in June 1931 as a guarantee against a French loan of 6 million to the infant Republic. As Sardà points out, the new monetary authorities still lacked what classical economists would consider adequate backing for Spain's fiduciary circulation. Thus the New Order embarked, at a moment of great uncertainty, on a system of 'managed money'. The dangers of inflation were considerable (Sardà, 1970).

There is complete agreement among present-day Spanish economists that from 1942 until the Stabilisation Plan of 1959 Spain was without a coherent set of monetary policies. Raimundo Poveda contends that practically the only function of the country's financial system at this time was to provide the real economy, not least the public sector, with whatever funds it required. Ministers insisted that monetary factors should not constitute an obstacle to the regime's paramount objective of rapid industrialisation (Poveda, 1980).

What role did the financial institutions play during this era of permissive monetary policy? The Bank of Spain, while nominally a private entity with its own shareholders, remained under the control of the Ministry of Finance. This subordinate position was reinforced by the Banking Act (*Ley de Ordenación Bancaria*) of December 1946. One of the central bank's main functions was to implement an almost permanent policy of cheap money. For most of the 1940s the Bank's rediscount rate hovered around three per cent. On the eve of the so-called pre-stabilisation measures of July 1957 it stood at 4.25 per cent. Apart from interest rate policy, the Spanish authorities paid scant regard to the use of monetary instruments, preferring instead to intervene directly in nearly every aspect of production and distribution through a mixed bag of controls (Sardà, 1970; Gonzàlez, 1979).

One peculiar feature of Spanish monetary policy before 1959, attacked by Sardà, was the regime's idiosyncratic separation of foreign and domestic operations. The former were handed over in August 1939 to a new organisation, the *Instituto Español de Moneda Extranjera*. In line with the interventionist ideology of the New State, the IEME was placed under the auspices, not of the more orthodox Finance Ministry, but rather that hothouse of autarkic policies and import substitution, the Ministry of Industry and Commerce. Fernando Eguidazu tells how, from 1948 until its demise in July 1959, the IEME extended and manipulated Spain's cumbersome system of multiple exchange rates for specific imports and exports (Sardà, 1970; Eguidazu, 1978).

The most criticised aspect of Spain's commercial banks (*bancas privadas*) during the period 1939–62 was the existence of a *numerus clausus* on new entrants. As part of their aim to control wartime finances, in August 1936 the Nationalists placed a ban on the creation of any further financial institutions. This restrictive legislation, known as the 'status quo', was retained by the New State after the ceasefire and later ratified by the 1946 Banking Act. In a unique study on the power of the Spanish banks, Juan Muñoz charts the growing importance of the financial oligarchy which, helped by the status quo legislation, absorbed a number of its smaller competitors. During the 1940s, the five largest commercial banks (Bilbao, Vizcaya, Hispano Americano, Español de Crédito and Central) expanded at unprecedented rates, while their profits increased sevenfold. Over the next decade the profits of the 'big five' more than quadrupled from 440 million pesetas to 1,891 millions. Between 1940 and 1960, their combined reserves jumped from next to nothing to 7,472 million pesetas. More disturbingly, credit restrictions in force during the 1950s enabled the leading financial institutions to gain an almost total monopoly over the financing of domestic industry. Spanish companies independent of the banks, Muñoz tells us, more or less disappeared (Muñoz, 1969).

Reform, crisis and liberalisation

The collapse of the Franco regime's autarkic policies in the late 1950s, because of galloping inflation and the depletion of Spain's gold and foreign currency reserves, is outlined in Chapter 2. Among other objectives, the Stabilisation Plan of 1959 attempted to eradicate what the technocrats saw as the main cause of recent inflation: the massive increase in the issue of public debt, most of which was absorbed by the financial system, to pay for the government's reconstructionist projects. On this subject, Poveda stresses the simple and direct approach of the monetary authorities. Lacking the skills required to pursue more sophisticated policies, Spain's monetary authorities set about imposing savage cuts in public expenditure, raised interest rates and increased taxes. Since they had little understanding as to how far to proceed along these lines, the short-term result of their intervention was the economic downturn of 1960. Sardà, for his part, attributes the long-run success of the Stabilisation Plan to the profound psychological shock it administered to the country, whose effects were immediate and spectacular (Sardà, 1970; Poveda, 1980).

By common consent, Spain's outmoded and highly-protected financial institutions also needed a major shake up. However, as Poveda contends, the process of liberalisation, although incorporated into the Stabilisation Plan with regard to foreign trade, was not extended to the realms of finance. Despite official claims that new legislation led to far-reaching structural changes in the financial sector, there is little evidence to demonstrate these assertions. Nothing indicates that Spain's monetary authorities in the 1960s believed in the virtues of the market. Indeed, the opposite is true: government intervention in the every-day activities of the financial system increased. All that changed, according to Poveda, was that whereas before 1959 the banks were required by the state to fund public-sector schemes on the most favourable terms, in the era of Development priority status was granted to those sectors singled out for special treatment by the development plans (Poveda, 1980).

After much deliberation, the Franco regime announced the reform of the financial system in an Act of April 1962. Among the changes which it introduced were the nationalisation of the Bank of Spain and the scrapping of the much-derided status quo legislation. In reality, however, little practical resulted from these initiatives. Apart from the elimination of its private shareholders, and the new responsibility which it acquired for external monetary policy, the central bank functioned much as before (Poveda, 1980). In terms of domestic monetary policy, most analysts characterise official attitudes as still essentially permissive. José Miguel Andreu distinguishes the period 1959–69 as initiating a switch in the Bank of Spain's overall strategy from an emphasis on interest rate policy to an attempt to control the money supply. Even so, this transitional phase in Spanish monetary policy was characterised by a lack of conviction on the part of the authorities. Only after 1970, Andreu maintains, did Spain achieve more controlled monetary growth (Andreu, 1989–90).

With regard to the commercial banks, Poveda contends that the 1962 Act suffered from the fact that its two main aims – to stimulate medium and long-term investment and to curb the influence of the banks in the finance of industry – were mutually contradictory. Moreover, notwithstanding the abolition of the notorious 'status quo' measure, the imposition of additional regulations and conditions on banking practice, meant that the formation of new financial institutions was far from straightforward. Furthermore, an attempt to divide the commercial banks into industrial and retail banks was frustrated by the banks which preferred to remain mixed (Poveda, 1980; Ontiveros and Valero, 1989).

Between 1978 and 1985, the Spanish banking system was massively shaken by a crisis without parallel in the western world. According to Emilio Ontiveros and Francisco Valero, of the 110 Spanish banks operating in 1977, over half collapsed, including twenty banks in the Rumasa group. The banking crisis, which reflected the general economic malaise of the period, was most pronounced among the smaller and more recently established institutions. Such banks, these authors argue, not only lacked professional expertise but also took the gravest risks. Together they accounted for 27 per cent of all the banks' resources, 28 per cent of employees and 19 per cent of branches. Álvaro Cuervo's conservative estimates of the direct costs of the bank collapses, at constant 1985 prices, is a staggering 1,581 billion pesetas, of which the Rumasa group was responsible for 718 billions. To tackle the crisis, in November 1977 the Suárez administration set up the *Fondo de Garantía de Depósitos*, to safeguard the position of depositors. The big banks were also forced to take part in the rescue operations (Ontiveros and Valero, 1988; Cuervo, 1988).

In his account of the banking system of modern Spain, Salmon analyses the processes of liberalisation and modernisation (above all the adoption of new technology), which got underway in the late 1970s and were aimed at bringing the country into line with the norms and practices of western Europe. Notwithstanding recent mergers, he argues, Spanish banks remain small and inefficient by world standards. As late as 1989, only the newly amalgamated Banco Bilbao Vizcaya was ranked in the world's top hundred financial institutions. Elsewhere, liberalising measures introduced in 1977 allowed Spain's savings banks (*cajas de ahorro*) to compete on similar terms with the commercial banks. During the period 1979–89 their share of total deposits increased from 33 per cent to nearly 46 per cent. In addition, after 1978, foreign banks were also permitted to open full branches in Spain. By 1987, according to Ontiveros and Valero, fifty foreign banks operated south of the Pyrenees, including ten Spanish banks which were foreign controlled (Ontiveros and Valero, 1988; Salmon, 1991).

Concluding remarks

After the troubled times of the Spanish Civil War, followed by a decade of stagnation in the 1940s, the second half of the twentieth century has witnessed long periods of fairly rapid economic growth south of the Pyrenees. Since the 1950s, Spain has been transformed from a backward agrarian nation to a modern industrial society with a constantly expanding service sector. The false goals of autarky and import substitution were eventually replaced by an unswerving commitment to a more open economy based on trade liberalisation, inward investment and mass tourism. Since 1986, the country has been an active member of the European Economic Community. To the surprise and acclaim of many commentators, Felipe González's Spain joined the exchange rate mechanism of the European Monetary System ahead of Margaret Thatcher's Britain. Something approximating the full benefits of EC membership can be expected to materialise when the single European market comes into operation after 31 December 1992. Yet, even the most optimistic forecasts calculate that it will take at least another twenty years before per capita incomes in Spain attain the average of the European Community as presently constituted.

Five centuries after Christopher Columbus set sail from the tiny Andalusian port of Palos de la Frontera to initiate what is nowadays commonly referred to as Spain's encounter with the New World, the Spanish authorities looked forward to 1992 as possibly constituting another *annus mirabilis*. The Seville World Trade Exhibition, Barcelona's staging of the Olympic Games and Madrid's designation as Europe's cultural capital were viewed in government circles as setting the seal on Spain's remarkable process of economic development and political transformation from dictatorship to democracy. Such ventures, it was hoped, would also bring in vital revenue from the crowds of visitors who flooded in from all corners of the globe. Official optimism, coupled with much private greed, contrasted with a fair degree of cynicism, not least from many of Spain's two-and-a-half million unemployed and a younger generation stymied in its ambitions. Moreover, not all of the regions of the peninsula were scheduled to share in the anticipated bonanza of 1992.

The previous chapters are intended as a brief synthesis, largely based on Spanish sources, of the principal aspects of economic activity since the Civil War. In such an approach, I am all too conscious that economic analysis may get too neatly divorced from its ideological and historical framework. Whatever positive results the Franco dictatorship achieved in the economic sphere must be set against the regime's political illegitimacy and its disdain for the democratic process. Although personally critical of the gradualist economic policies of the Suárez administration in the late 1970s in the face of the world recession, I freely admit that the overriding issue of the day was an attempt to construct democracy against the background of a brooding military and a 'bunkered' establishment. With regard to the performance of the Socialist government since 1982, there can be little room for dissension from the consensus opinion that Finance Ministers Boyer and Solchaga have enjoyed considerable success in strictly economic terms, unemployment excepted. Yet where is the concern for ordinary people, the commitment to social justice and the willingness to take on powerful vested interests which marked the early years of the Second Republic? The González administration may have temporarily balanced the books, but it has done precious little to satisfy the needs and objectives of those Spaniards who voted for it, albeit in dwindling numbers, in successive elections since 1982.

Bibliography

Albarracín, J. and Yago, A. (1986). 'La industria española en el período 1970 a 1984', *Boletín Económico (Banco de España)*, February, 21–30.

Albentosa, L. (1985). 'La política de ajuste: reconversión industrial', *Información Comercial Española*, 617–8, 175–91.

Alonso, J. A. (1988). 'El sector exterior', in J. L. García Delgado (ed.), *España: economía* (Madrid), pp. 273–365.

Alsina, R. (1987). 'Estrategia de desarrollo en España, 1964–75: planes y realidad', *Cuadernos de Economía*, 15, 337–70.

Anderson, C. W. (1970). *The Political Economy of Spain: Policy Making in an Authoritarian System* (Madison).

Andreu, J. M. (1989–90). 'Un análisis de la política monetaria española, 1939–89', *Información Comercial Española*, 676–7 (ii), 3–19.

Arango, J. (1987). 'La modernización demográfica de la sociedad española', in J. Nadal, A. Carreras and C. Sudrià (eds), *La economía española en el siglo xx: una perspectiva histórica* (Barcelona), pp. 201–36.

Arroyo Ilera, F. (1988). *El reto de Europa: España en la CEE* (Madrid).

Banco Bilbao Vizcaya (1990). *Situación, 1990: The Spanish Economy in 1989 and 1990* (Bilbao).

(1991). 'La economía española en 1990', *Situación* 1990 (3).

(1992). *Situación 1991: The Spanish Economy in 1990 and 1991* (Bilbao).

Barceló, L. V. (1987). 'La modernización de la agricultura española y el bienestar', *Información Comercial Española*, 652, 13–27.

Barciela, C. (1981). 'El estraperlo de trigo en la posguerra', *Moneda y Crédito*, 159, 17–37.

(1986). 'Los costes del franquismo en el sector agrario: la ruptura del proceso de transformaciones', in R. Garrabou, C. Barciela and J. I. Jiménez Blanco (eds), *Historia agraria de la España contemporánea. 3. El fin de la agricultura tradicional* (Barcelona), pp. 383–454.

Bardají, I., Díaz Berenguer, J., Sumpsi, J. M. and Tió, C. (1982). 'Nuevas perspectivas de la política agraria en España', *Agricultura y Sociedad*, 24, 257–318.

Bernal, A. M. (1985). 'La llamada crisis finisecular, 1872–1919', in J. L. García Delgado (ed.), *La España de la Restauración; política económica, legislación y cultura: I Coloquio de Segovia sobre historia contemporánea de España* (Madrid), pp. 215–63.

(1991). 'Resistencias al cambio económico en el sector agrícola, 1880–1930', in J. L. García Delgado (ed.), *España entre dos siglos, 1875–1931: continuidad y cambio* (Madrid), pp. 141–56.

Braña, F., Buesa, M. and Molero, J. (1979). 'El fin de le etapa nacionalista: industrialización y dependencia en España, 1951–9', *Investigaciones Económicas*, 9, 151–217.

(1983). 'El estado en los procesos de industrialización atrasada: notas acerca del caso español, 1939–77', *El Trimestre Económico*, 197, 85–116.

(1984). *El estado y el cambio tecnológico en la industrialización tardía: un análisis del caso español* (Mexico City).

Carreras, A. (1984). 'La producción industrial española, 1842–1981: construcción de un índice anual', *Revista de Historia Económica*, 2(i), 127–57.

(1987). 'La industria: atraso y modernización', in Nadal, Carreras and Sudrià (eds), *op. cit.*, pp. 280–312.

(1989). 'Depresión económica y cambio estructural durante el decenio bélico, 1936–45', in J. L. García Delgado (ed.), *El primer franquismo: España durante la segunda guerra mundial: V Coloquio de Historia Contemporánea de España* (Madrid), pp. 3–33.

Catalán, J. (1989). 'Autarquía y desarrollo de la industria fabril durante la segunda guerra mundial: un enfoque comparativo', in García Delgado (ed.), *El primer franquismo*, pp. 35–88.

Clavera, J., Esteban, J. M., Monés, M. A., Montserrat, A. and Ros Hombravella, J. (1978). *Capitalismo español: de la autarquía a la estabilización, 1939–59* (Barcelona).

Comín, F. (1986). 'El presupuesto del estado tras la Guerra Civil: dos pasos atrás', *Economistas*, 21, 24–32.

Cuadrado, J. R. (1988). 'El sector servicios: evolución, características y perspectivas de futuro', in García Delgado (ed.), *España*, pp. 231–70.

(1990). 'La expansión de los servicios en el contexto del cambio estructural de la economía española', *Papeles de Economía Española*, 42, 98–120.

Cuervo, A. (1988). *La crisis bancaria en España, 1977–85* (Barcelona).

Díez Nicolás, J. (1971). 'La transición demográfica en España, 1900–60', *Revista de Estudios Sociales*, 1, 89–118.

(1985a). 'Familia y fecundidad en España', *Desarrollo*, 1, 36–43.

(1985b). 'La mortalidad en la Guerra Civil Española', *Boletín de la Asociación de Demografía Histórica*, 3, 41–55.

Donges, J. (1971). 'From an Autarkic towards a Cautious Outward-

Looking Industrialisation Policy: the Case of Spain', *Weltwirtschaftliches Archiv*, 107, 33–72.

(1976). *La industrialización en España: políticas, logros, perspectivas* (Vilassar de Mar).

(1983). 'Anotaciones sobre competitividad de las exportaciones españolas', *Información Comercial Española*, 604, 59–61.

Eguidazu, F. (1978). *Intervención monetaria y control de cambios en España, 1900–77* (Madrid).

Estapé, F. and Amado, M. (1986). 'Realida y propaganda de la planificación indicativa en España', in J. Fontana (ed.), *España bajo el franquismo* (Barcelona), pp. 206–14.

Fanjul, E. (1980). 'El papel de la ayuda americana en la economía española, 1951–7', *Información Comercial Española*, 577, 159–65.

Fanjul, O., Maravall, F., Pérez Prim, J. M. and Segura, J. (1975). *Cambios en la estructura interindustrial de la economía española, 1962–70: una primera aproximación* (Madrid).

Fontana, J. and Nadal, J. (1976). 'Spain, 1914–70', in C. M. Cipolla (ed.), *The Fontana Economic History of Europe*, 6 (ii) (London), pp. 460–529.

Fuchs, V. R. (1968). *The Service Economy* (New York).

Fuentes Quintana, E. (1984). 'El Plan de Estabilización económica, veinticinco años después', *Información Comercial Española*, 612–13, 25–40.

(1986). 'La economía española desde el Plan de Estabilización de 1959: el papel del sector exterior', in T. Martínez Vara (ed.), *Mercado y desarrollo económico en la España contemporánea* (Madrid), pp. 131–57.

(1988). 'Tres decenios de la economía española en perspectiva', in García Delgado (ed.), *España*, pp. 1–75.

Fuentes Quintana, E. and Requeijo, J. (1984). 'La larga marcha hacia la política económica inevitable', *Papeles de Economía Española*, 21, 3–39.

Fusi, J. P. (1985). *Franco: autoritarismo y poder personal* (Madrid).

Gámir, L. (1980). 'El período 1939–59: la autarquía y la política de estabilización', in L. Gámir (ed.), *Política económica de España*, third ed. (Madrid), pp. 13–30.

García Alonso, J. M. (1983). 'La energía en la economía española: una visión de conjunto', *Papeles de Economía Española*, 14, 2–13.

García Delgado, J. L. (1984). 'La industrialización española en el primer tercio del siglo xx', in J. M. Jover (ed.), *Los comienzos del siglo xx*, vol. 37 of *Historia de España Menéndez Pidal* (Madrid), pp. 1–171.

(1986). 'Estancamiento industrial e intervencionismo económico durante el primer franquismo', in Fontana (ed.), *España bajo el franquismo*, pp. 170–91.

(1987). 'La industrialización y el desarrollo económico de España durante el franquismo', in Nadal, Carreras and Sudrià (eds), *op. cit.*, pp. 164–89.

García Delgado, J. L. and Muñoz Cidad, C. (1988). 'La agricultura: cambios estructurales en los últimos decenios', in García Delgado (ed.), *España*, pp. 119–52.

Gómez Mendoza, A. (1986). 'La industria de la construcción residencial: Madrid, 1820–1935', *Moneda y Crédito*, 177, 53–81.

González, M.-J. (1979). *La economía política del franquismo, 1940–70: dirigismo, mercado y planificación* (Madrid).

Grupo de Estudios de Historia Rural (1983). 'Notas sobre la producción agraria española, 1891–1931', *Revista de Historia Económica*, 1 (i), 185–252.

Harrison, J. (1985). *The Spanish Economy in the Twentieth Century* (London and Sydney).

(1991). 'Towards the Liberalization of the Spanish Economy, 1951–9', in C. Holmes and A. Booth (eds), *Economy and Society: European Industrialisation and its Social Consequences: Essays Presented to Sidney Pollard* (Leicester), pp. 102–15.

International Bank for Reconstruction and Development (1963). *The Economic Development of Spain* (Baltimore).

Iranzo Martín, J. E. (1984). 'El sector energético español: realidades y posibilidades', *Papeles de Economía Española*, 21, 271–89.

Jiménez Blanco, J. I. (1986). Introduction to Garrabou, Barciela and Jiménez Blanco (eds), *op. cit.*, pp. 9–141.

Jiménez Latorre, F. and de Guindos Jurado, L. (1985). 'Algunos efectos económicos de la inversión extranjera en España', *Información Comercial Española*, 624–5, 39–51.

Leal, J. L., Leguina, J., Naredo, J. M. and Tarrafeta, L. (1975). *La agricultura en el desarrollo capitalista español* (Madrid).

López de Sebastián, J. (1970). *Política agraria en España, 1920–70* (Madrid).

Maluquer, J. (1987). 'De la crisis colonial a la guerra europea: veinte años de economía española', in Nadal, Carreras and Sudrià (eds), *op. cit.*, pp. 62–104.

Maravall, F. (1976). *Crecimiento, dimensión y concentración de empresas industriales españolas, 1964–73* (Madrid).

Marín Quemada, J. M. (1978). *Política petrolífera española* (Madrid).

Martí, L. (1989–90). 'Estabilización y desarrollo', *Información Comercial Española*, 676–7 (ii), 67–79.

Martín, C., Romero, L. R. and Segura, J. (1981). *Cambios en la estructura interindustrial española, 1962–75* (Madrid).

Martín Aceña, P. (1991). 'Los problemas monetarios al término de la guerra civil', *Papeles de Trabajo, Instituto Universitario Ortega y Gasset* (Madrid).

Martín Aceña, P. and Comín, F. (1991). *INI: 50 años de industrialización en España* (Madrid).

Martínez Serrano, J. A., Mas Ivars, M., Paricio Torregrosa, J. Pérez García, F., Queseda Ibáñez, J., and Reig Martínez, E. (1982). *Economía española, 1960–80: crecimiento y cambio estructural* (Madrid).

Merigó, E. (1982). 'Spain', in A. Boltho (ed.), *The European Economy: Growth and Crisis* (Oxford), pp. 554–80.

Muns, J. (1986). *Historia de las relaciones entre España y el Fondo Monetario Internacional, 1958–82: veinticinco años de economía española* (Madrid).

Muñoz, J. (1969). *El poder de la banca en España* (Madrid).

Myro, R. (1988). 'La industria: expansión, crisis y reconversión', in García Delgado (ed.), *España*, pp. 197–230.

Naredo, J. M. (1974). *La evolución de la agricultura en España: desarrollo capitalista y crisis de las formas de producción tradicionales*, second edn (Barcelona).

(1981). 'La incidencia del estraperlo en la economía de las grandes fincas del sur', *Agricultura y Sociedad*, 19, 81–115.

(1986). 'La agricultura en el desarrollo económico', in Garrabou, Barciela and Jiménez Blanco (eds), *op. cit.*, pp. 455–98.

(1988). 'Diez años de agricultura española', *Agricultura y Sociedad*, 46, 9–36.

Navarro Arancegui, M. (1989). 'La política de reconversión industrial en España', *Información Comercial Española*, 666, 45–69.

Navarro Rubio, M. (1991). *Mis memorias: testimonio de una vida política truncada por el 'caso MATESA'* (Barcelona).

Nicolau, R. (1989). 'La población', in A. Carreras (ed.), *Estadísticas históricas de España: siglos xix–xx* (Madrid), pp. 51–91.

Ontiveros, E. and Valero, F. J. (1988). 'El sistema financiero: instituciones y funcionamiento', in García Delgado (ed.), *España*, pp. 367–429.

Payne, S. (1987). *The Franco Regime, 1936–75* (Madison).

Pérez Blanco, J. M. (1983). 'Rasgos macroeconómicos básicos de la evolución de la agricultura española, 1964–82; crisis actual', *Papeles de Economía Española*, 16, 2–21.

Poveda, R. (1980). 'Política monetaria y financiera', in Gámir (ed.), *op. cit.*, pp. 33–75.

Ribas i Massana, A. (1978). *L'economia catalana sota el franquisme, 1939–53* (Barcelona).

Rivero, P. (1989). 'Análisis de la política energética en España', *Boletín de Estudios Económicos*, 137, 227–37.

Rodríguez de Pablo, J. (1988). 'La inversión extranjera en la economía española y los movimientos internacionales de capital', *Boletín Económico (Banco de España)*, May, 83–97.

Rojo, L. A. (1987). 'La crisis de la economía española, 1973–84', in Nadal, Carreras and Sudrià (eds), *op. cit.*, pp. 190–200.

Ros Hombravella, J. (1979). *Política económica española, 1959–73* (Barcelona).

Rubio Jiménez, M. (1968). 'El Plan de Estabilización de 1959', *Moneda y Crédito*, 105, 3–38.

Sáez, F. (1990). 'El empleo en las actividades de servicios', *Papeles de Economía Española*, 42, 123–36.

Salmon, K. G. (1991). *The Modern Spanish Economy: Transformation and Integration into Europe* (London).

San Juan Mesonada, C. and Romo Lagunas, M. J. (1987). 'Evolución intercensal de las explotaciones agrarias, 1962–1972–1982', *Agricultura y Sociedad*, 44, 137–68.

Sardà, J. (1970). 'El Banco de España, 1931–62', Servicio de Estudios del Banco de España, *El Banco de España: una historia económica* (Madrid), pp. 421–79.

Schwartz, P. and González, M.-J. (1978). *Una historia del Instituto Nacional de Industria, 1941–76* (Madrid).

Sudrià, C. (1987). 'Un factor determinante: la energía', in Nadal, Carreras and Sudrià (eds), *op cit.*, pp. 313–63.

(1988a). 'Energia', in *Història econòmica de la Catalunya contemporània*, vol. 5 (Barcelona), pp. 211–80.

(1988b). 'El sector energético: condicionamientos y posibilidades', in García Delgado (ed.), *España*, pp. 177–96.

Sumpsi, J. M. (1983). 'La política agraria, 1968–82', *Papeles de Economía Española*, 16, 322–34.

Tamames, R. (1970). *Estructura económica de España* (Madrid).

(1973). *La República: la era de Franco* (Madrid).

(1989–90). 'Los planes de desarrollo, 1964–75', *Información Comercial Española*, 676–7 (ii), 57–65.

Tedde, P. (1986). 'Economía y franquismo: a propósito de una biografía', *Revista de Historia Económica*, 4, 627–37.

Tezanos, J. F. (1989). 'Modernización y cambio social en España', in J. F. Tezanos, R. Cotarelo and A. Blas (eds), *La transición democrática española* (Madrid), pp. 63–115.

Thomas, H. (1977). *The Spanish Civil War*, third edn (Harmondsworth).

Tió, C. (1982). *La política de aceites comestibles en la España del siglo xx* (Madrid).

Tortella, G. (1984). 'La agricultura en la economía de la España contemporánea, 1830–1930', *Papeles de Economía Española*, 20, 62–75.

(1986). 'Sobre el significado histórico del franquismo', *Revista de Occidente*, 59, 104–14.

Tusell, J. (1988). *La dictadura de Franco* (Madrid).

Varela, M. (1989–90). 'El plan de desarrollo como yo lo recuerdo', *Información Comercial Española*, 676–7 (i), 41–55.

Velasco, C. (1982). 'El pensamiento agrario y la apuesta industrializadora en la España de los cuarenta', *Agricultura y Sociedad*, 23, 233–73.

(1984). 'El ingenierismo como directriz básica de la política económica durante la autarquía, 1936–51', *Información Comercial Española*, 606, 97–106.

(1988). 'El origen militar de la autarquía y su significación económica', *Perspectiva Contemporánea*, 1, 117–33.

Viñas, A. (1981). *Los pactos secretos de Franco con Estados Unidos: bases, ayuda económica, recortes de soberanía* (Barcelona).

(1982). 'La primera ayuda económica norteamericana a España', in *Lecturas de economía española: 50 aniversario del Cuerpo de Técnicos Oficiales del Estado* (Madrid), pp. 49–90.

(1984). *Guerra, dinero, dictadura: ayuda fascista y autarquía en la España de Franco* (Barcelona).

Viñas, A., Viñuela, J., Eguidazu, F., Pulgar, C. F. and Florensa, S. (1979). *Política exterior de España, 1931–75*, 2 vols (Madrid).

Whealey, R. H. (1977). 'How Franco Financed his War – Reconsidered', *Journal of Contemporary History*, 12, 133–52.

Index

agriculture
   agrarian reform 1, 4
   concentration of holdings 28–31
   fertilisers 8, 26, 28
   irrigation 6, 8, 28
   mechanisation 3, 26–30
aircraft production 6, 36, 40
Algeciras 45
Algeria 45
Andalusia 3, 24, 52
Aragon 3
Arburúa, Manuel 10–11, 28, 53
Argentina 9
armed forces 1, 8, 17, 26, 68
Asturias 5, 43, 52
Australia 49
autarky 5, 8–9, 11, 26, 33–5, 37, 42,
   53–4, 56, 62, 63, 67
automobiles 6, 35, 36, 40, 55

Balearic Islands 52
Bank of Spain 11, 12, 17, 60, 62, 64
banking 62–6
Barcelona 5, 6, 21, 25, 45, 52, 67
Basque Country 1, 5, 8, 24, 44, 52
Belgium 21, 23, 49
Bilbao 5, 45
birth rate 20, 22
black market 2, 8, 10, 27, 29
Boyer, Miguel 18, 68
Burgos 61

Canada 49
Canary Islands 23, 32, 52
Cánovas, Cirilo 28
Cantabria 23, 52

Castellón 45
Catalonia 1, 7, 23, 24, 37, 44, 45, 52
Cavestany, Rafael 27, 28
cement 6, 14, 34, 35, 39, 44
cereals 4, 9, 28, 31
chemicals 7, 34, 36, 37, 38, 39, 44
civil guard 3, 27
coal 5, 36, 43–7
Communist Party 17
construction industry 6, 38
Corunna 45
Cuba 3
Cuenca 21

dairy farming 28, 31
Development Plans 12–16, 47, 64
drought 7–8, 26, 44

economic nationalism 5, 35, 53
education 23, 49, 51
electrical goods 16, 40, 41
electricity supply 6, 36, 42–8
emigrant remittances 4, 14, 24, 57–8
emigration 1, 2, 21, 23, 24
energy 6, 10, 14, 16, 29, 33, 34, 38,
   42–8, 56
Escombreras 45
European Community (EC) 19, 31,
   41, 46, 51, 54–7, 67
European Free Trade Area
   (EFTA) 54, 55
European Monetary System (EMS)
   67
exports
   foodstuffs 32
   manufactures 36, 37, 38, 41, 53

Extremadura 24

foodstuffs industry 5, 38
footwear 16, 40, 41, 55
foreign investment 5, 12, 13, 14, 35,
    38, 53, 57, 58, 65–6
foros 4
France 3, 15, 18, 21, 23, 32, 39, 61
Franco, Gen. Francisco 1, 8, 10, 11,
    13, 17, 19, 23, 27, 43, 47, 61, 68
furniture 5, 55

Galicia 23, 24, 52
García Ortiz, Juan Antonio 11
gasógeno 43
General Agreement on Tariffs and
    Trade (GATT) 54, 55
González, Felipe 18, 41, 67–8
Greece 7
Guadalajara 21, 45

health services 49
horticulture 3, 32
hotels 51
Huelva 45
hunger 2, 3, 21, 26, 29
hydro-electric power 43, 45

imports
    capital goods 10, 14, 33, 34, 37,
        53, 56
    foodstuffs 9, 14, 31
    manufactures 14, 37
    raw materials 9, 10, 13, 33, 34, 53,
        56
    substitution 8, 10, 34, 47, 53, 62,
        67
industrial restructuring 18, 40–1
Instituto Español de Moneda
    Extranjera (IEME) 62
Instituto Nacional de Industria (INI)
    35, 36, 37, 41, 43
International Monetary Fund (IMF)
    12, 54
Italy 1, 7, 21, 35–6, 39

Japan 13, 39

Larraz, José 61
latifundios 3, 4, 28–30
Latin America 2, 4, 23

León 31
livestock 3, 28, 31
López Bravo, Gregorio 14
López Rodó, Laureano 11, 14
Lugo 21
Luxembourg Accord 55, 56

machine tools 40
Madrid 6, 21, 24, 34, 52, 67
Málaga 25
Marshall Aid 9, 10
mergers 38, 41
metallurgy 5
minifundios 3, 4, 28
mining 5, 34
Moncloa Pacts 17, 18
Movimiento 1
Murcia 24, 52

natural gas 45, 47
Navarro Rubio, Mariano 11, 54
Negrín, Juan 60
Netherlands 21
New Castile 24, 52
Newly-Industrialising Countries
    (NICs) 16, 40
nuclear power 45, 47

oil 14, 16, 18, 34, 36, 42–7, 57
Old Castile 2, 24, 31
olives 2, 19, 26
oranges 3, 27
Organisation for Economic
    Cooperation and Development
    (OECD) 12, 13, 15, 49, 51, 54,
    55, 56, 57, 58
Organisation of Petroleum Exporting
    Countries (OPEC) 14, 42, 46

País Valenciano 3
papermaking 5
Perón, Gen. Juan 9
peseta 4, 5, 9, 11, 12, 17, 37, 56, 58
plastics 40
potatoes 3
Primo de Rivera, Gen. Miguel 5, 6
protectionism 2, 4, 5, 8, 9, 10, 12,
    13, 19, 37, 53–5
public works 6
publishing 5
Puertollano 45

railways 5, 6
rationing 2
rice growing 28, 29, 31
roads 6, 9
Rumasa 65

Saragossa 25
Sardà, Juan 11
Second Republic 1, 2, 6, 60, 61
services 13, 23, 24, 49–52
Seville 25, 67
shipbuilding 5, 14, 16, 36, 40, 41, 44
Socialist Party 18, 19, 41, 47, 68
Solchaga, Carlos 18, 68
Soria 21
Soviet Union 60
Spanish Civil War 1, 2, 4, 6, 20–3,
    27, 42, 57, 60, 68
Spanish Lobby 9
Stabilisation Plan 10–14, 33, 37, 50,
    53, 54, 57, 62, 63, 64
status quo legislation 63, 64
Suanzes, Juan Antonio 35, 36
Suárez, Adolfo 17, 18, 41, 65, 68
sugar beet 3
Switzerland 23

taxation 12, 13, 15, 36, 38, 41, 46,
    58, 63
Teruel 21

Texaco 43
textiles 4–5, 7, 16, 35, 37, 40, 41
Tokyo Round 55
tourism 14, 38, 49–52, 57–8, 67
trade unions 1, 18, 37, 39, 41
transport 43, 44, 49, 51, 52

Ullastres, Alberto 11, 37, 54
unemployment 17, 18, 24, 39–40,
    41, 50, 51, 68
United Kingdom 39, 49, 67
United Nations 8, 43
United States 9, 10, 11, 33, 39, 43,
    49, 53
urbanisation 2, 6, 21, 24–5, 42, 50

Valencia 25, 34, 52
Varela, Manuel 11
vegetables 4, 19, 56
Venezuela 23
viticulture 2, 28
Vizcaya 5, 6, 21

West Germany 23, 39
wheat 2, 26, 27, 29, 30, 31
World Bank 12, 15, 36, 54

Yugoslavia 7

Zamora 21

New Studies in Economic and Social History

Titles in the series available from Cambridge University Press:

1. M. Anderson
    Approaches to the history of the Western family, 1500–1914

2. W. Macpherson
    The economic development of Japan, 1868–1941

3. R. Porter
    Disease, medicine, and society in England: second edition

4. B.W.E. Alford
    British economic performance since 1945

5. A. Crowther
    Social policy in Britain, 1914–1939

6. E. Roberts
    Women's work 1840–1940

7. C. O'Grada
    The great Irish famine

8. R. Rodger
    Housing in urban Britain 1780–1914

9. P. Slack
    The English Poor Law 1531–1782

10. J.L. Anderson
    Explaining long-term economic change

11. D. Baines
    Emigration from Europe 1815–1930

12. M. Collins
    Banks and industrial finance 1800–1939

13. A. Dyer
    Decline and growth in English towns 1400–1640

14. R.B. Outhwaite
    Dearth, public policy and social disturbance in England, 1550–1800

15. M. Sanderson
    Education, economic change and society in England

16. R.D. Anderson
    Universities and elites in Britain since 1800

17. C. Heywood
    The development of the French economy, 1700–1914

18. R.A. Houston
    The population history of Britain and Ireland 1500–1750

19. A.J. Reid
    Social classes and social relations in Britain 1850–1914

20. R. Woods
    The population of Britain in the nineteenth century

21. T.C. Barker
    The rise and rise of road transport, 1700–1990

22. J. Harrison
    The Spanish economy

23. C. Schmitz
    The growth of big business in the United States and Western Europe, 1850–1939

24. R.A. Church
    The rise and decline of the British motor industry

25. P. Horn
    Children's work and welfare, 1780–1880

26. R. Perren
    Agriculture in depression, 1870–1940

27. R.J. Overy
    The Nazi economic recovery 1932–1938: second edition

Previously published as

Studies in Economic History

Titles in the series available from the Macmillan Press Limited

1. B.W.E. Alford
   Depression and recovery? British economic growth, 1918–1939

2. M. Anderson
   Population change in north-western Europe, 1750–1850

3. S.D. Chapman
   The cotton industry in the industrial revolution: second edition

4. N. Charlesworth
   British rule and the Indian economy, 1800–1914

5. L.A. Clarkson
   Proto-industrialisation: the first phase of industrialisation

6. D.C. Coleman
   Industry in Tudor and Stuart England

7. I.M. Drummond
   The gold standard and the international monetary system, 1900–1939

8. M.E. Falkus
   The industrialisation of Russia, 1700–1914

9. J.R. Harris
   The British iron industry, 1700–1850

10. J. Hatcher
    Plague, population and the English economy, 1348–1530

11. J.R. Hay
    The origins of the Liberal welfare reforms, 1906–1914

12. H. McLeod
    Religion and the working classes in nineteenth-century Britain

13. J.D. Marshall
    The Old Poor Law 1795–1834: second edition

14. R.J. Morris
    Class and class consciousness in the industrial revolution, 1750–1850

15. P.K. O'Brien
    The economic effects of the American civil war

16. P.L. Payne
    British entrepreneurship in the nineteenth century

17. G.C. Peden
    Keynes, the treasury and British economic policy

18. M.E. Rose
    The relief of poverty, 1834–1914

19. J. Thirsk
    England's agricultural regions and agrarian history, 1500–1750

20. J.R. Ward
    Poverty and progress in the Caribbean, 1800–1960

Economic History Society

The Economic History Society, which numbers around 3,000 members, publishes the *Economic History Review* four times a year (free to members) and holds an annual conference.

Enquiries about membership should be addressed to

The Assistant Secretary
Economic History Society
PO Box 70
Kingswood
Bristol
BS15 5TB

Full-time students may join at special rates.